Boyer & Valerie Coe's
Weight Training Book

Boyer & Valerie Coe's Weight Training Book

Boyer Coe & Valerie Coe

with Bill Reynolds

Contemporary Books, Inc.
Chicago

Library of Congress Cataloging in Publication Data

Coe, Boyer.
  Boyer and Valerie Coe's weight training book.

  Includes index.
  1. Bodybuilding.   2. Exercise.   I. Coe, Valerie.
II. Reynolds, Bill.   III. Title.   IV. Title: Bodybuilding book.
GV546.5.C63   1982   646.7′5   81-69605
ISBN 0-8092-5826-9   AACR2
ISBN 0-8092-5825-0 pbk.

All uncredited photos by John Balik.
Exercises photographed at Dan Howard's
  World Gym, Fountain Valley, California.
Competition photos courtesy of the IFBB.
Exercise photos printed by Isgo Lepejian,
  Burbank, California.

Published by Contemporary Books, Inc.
180 North Michigan Avenue, Chicago, Illinois 60601
Manufactured in the United States of America
Library of Congress Catalog Card Number: 81-69605
International Standard Book Number: 0-8092-5826-9 (cloth)
                                    0-8092-5825-0 (paper)

Published simultaneously in Canada by
Beaverbooks, Ltd.
150 Lesmill Road
Don Mills, Ontario M3B 2T5
Canada

Contents

Boyer Coe and Joe Weider, the Master Blaster, discuss Boyer's training

Foreword

by Joe Weider, Publisher, *Muscle & Fitness* magazine

During the past few years, weight training and bodybuilding have taken America and the rest of the world by storm. Today, three million American men and women train regularly with weights, more than five times the number who did so only five years ago! The increase in the number of women training with weights has been even more dramatic. More than 20 times as many women train regularly with weights now than did so five years ago!

There are numerous reasons for such rapid growth in weight training and bodybuilding. Chief among these is the tireless job that champion bodybuilders have done in promoting weight training as an ideal means of improving personal appearance, increasing athletic ability, improving health, and promoting a better self-image. And leading this group of athletes for the past few years has been the bodybuilding husband-and-wife team of Boyer and Valerie Coe.

For the sake of definition, weight training is exercising for any of several purposes with barbells, dumbbells, and a variety of weight resistance machines. Bodybuilding is a specialized subdivision of weight training in which the primary objective is to reshape the body. Body-building can range in intensity from being a mild activity aimed at reducing and toning a flabby area of the body to being an all-out effort to achieve competitive bodybuilding condition.

Many readers of this book will be interested in reshaping their bodies, but this is only one of ten benefits that can be attained from regular weight training. Here are the ten physical and psychological benefits that you can expect to receive if you follow the advice Boyer and Valerie Coe present in this book:

1. Improved physical fitness
2. Greater muscular strength
3. Body sculpture and reshaping
4. Improved health
5. Better sports performance
6. Relief from the tensions of everyday life
7. Improved muscle and joint flexibility
8. A more positive self-image and greater self-confidence
9. A new activity that you can do with your boyfriend, girlfriend, spouse, and/or children
10. A satisfying, competitive activity, which at the highest professional levels can become a source of considerable income

The Master Blaster (second from left) gave Valerie away at the Coe's wedding in 1980. *(Photo by Bill Reynolds)*

Bill Reynolds, Editor-in-Chief of *Muscle & Fitness,* and Joe Weider at Gold's Gym. *(Photo courtesy of Craig Dietz.)*

Boyer and Valerie Coe are eminently qualified to produce a book of this importance and magnitude, and they have done a wonderful job. Boyer and Valerie are high-level, competitive bodybuilders both as a couple and as individuals. They have repeatedly been finalists in the World Couples' Bodybuilding Championships. And in his distinguished 15-year bodybuilding career, Boyer Coe has won the Mr. America, Mr. International, Mr. World (five times), and Mr. Universe (four times) titles. He's been a finalist numerous times in the Mr. Olympia event (the professional world championships) and is a Professional World Cup Champion. Boyer holds the record for the highest point score ever achieved in professional bodybuilding competition.

The Coes are more than merely competitive bodybuilders, however. Collectively, they have close to 20 years of experience as gym and health spa owners and instructors. As such, they are thoroughly familiar with the problems and concerns of everyone who trains with weights.

The Coes are also popular authors of weight training and bodybuilding books and articles. Boyer has written three previous books: *Look Strong, Be Strong* (with Bob Summer), *Steroids* (with Dr. Stan Morey), and *Optimum Nutrition* (also with Dr. Stan Morey). Both have written scores of well-received articles over the years for *Muscle & Fitness*. In my considered opinion, no man-and-woman team in the field of weight training is as completely qualified to present weight training advice as Boyer and Valerie Coe.

I have read several drafts of this fine book and am convinced that it's the best overall weight training and bodybuilding book on the market. Boyer and Valerie Coe have spared no effort to include all of their experience and knowledge of weight training and bodybuilding in this authoritative, easily read, and informative volume. Follow their advice to the letter and you will soon be on the road to becoming a totally new and improved person!

Joe Weider
November 1981

Boyer & Valerie Coe's Weight Training Book

When Boyer Coe won the 1973 Professional Mr. Universe title, J. Paul Getty presented the trophy. The famous billionaire was a great supporter of international bodybuilding.

1
What's It All About?

Weight training and bodybuilding are good for every body, regardless of whether that body is male or female, young or old, in shape or out of shape, fat or thin, weak or strong. Weight training is even a superb physical fitness activity for handicapped men and women, as long as they have some use of their arms.

Weight training—or *progressive resistance exercise* as it is often called—is almost as old as recorded history. The first weight lifter was Milo of Croton, a wrestler of great repute in ancient Greece. Milo devised an exercise program in which he placed a calf across his shoulders and walked about a stadium with it each day. Naturally, the calf constantly grew in weight, and eventually Milo circled the stadium carrying a fully grown bull. Milo became so strong and physically fit from carrying his bull that he won six consecutive wrestling championships in the ancient Greek Olympic Games. Indeed, he was undefeated as a wrestler for 24 years.

Modern weight training is the same as Milo's crude form of working with gradually increasing resistance. Modern weight trainers and bodybuilders progressively add weight to their barbells, dumbbells, and exercise machines to be-

come stronger and better built.

When I started training, it was with a barbell and dumbbell set—not a calf—which was installed in my parents' garage in Lake Charles, Louisiana. I could do one repetition of a bench press movement (lying on my back and pushing a barbell from my chest to straight arms' length above my chest) with 65 pounds. Today I am capable of doing this same movement with nearly 500 pounds.

Valerie also started weight training in Louisiana, at the Boyer Coe Body Masters Gym in Metairie. In a squat movement (a deep knee bend with a barbell held across the shoulders) she could do only five repetitions with 40 pounds, while today she does five repetitions with four times as much weight in the same exercise.

So whether it is done with a calf or a set of weights, both men and women can remarkably improve their strength, appearance, health, and physical fitness through progressive resistance exercise. We have proved this on our own bodies and on the bodies of countless students.

Through most of American history, men and women have weight trained in one form or another. Light dumbbells were in common use

1

150 years ago, but only by men. Abraham Lincoln is said to have exercised regularly with dumbbells. Women, however, wouldn't have been caught dead near a barbell or dumbbell until the late 1960s and early 1970s. Even for men in the 19th century and early 20th century, lifting barbells and dumbbells for exercise and improved physical development was considered to be somewhat odd.

At the turn of the 20th century, Florenz Ziegfeld—who later gained everlasting fame as the producer of Ziegfeld's Follies—managed an obscure German strongman named Erwin Muller in a year-long vaudeville tour in America. Billed as Sandow, this athlete had used barbells and dumbbells to build great strength and a physique of classic beauty that would be impressive even by contemporary standards. Sandow exhibited so widely and was so universally admired by American men that he almost single-handedly fathered the bodybuilding movement for men in this country.

Early in the 20th century, Allan Calvert founded a factory that produced the world's first *adjustable* barbells and dumbbells, on which a variety of metal discs could be fitted to increase or decrease the weight of the apparatus. This was a great advance on previous barbells and dumbbells, which had been cast in fixed

Later in his career, Sandow displays just about everything else.

Sandow (age 21) displays his 16.6-inch right arm. His popularity began the bodybuilding movement in America.

Bernar MacFadden, editor of *Physical Culture,* strikes a classical pose.

Allan Calvert stands next to a display of adjustable dumbbells and barbells he manufactured.

poundages. Appropriately, Calvert christened his business the Milo Bar-Bell Company.

During the years before, during, and after World War I, Allan Calvert wrote numerous books and pamphlets to help popularize barbell and dumbbell training. Then the banner was taken up by Bernar MacFadden, who gave weight training much wider publicity with the many books he authored and with a magazine that he published. This magazine was variously called *Strength, Arena and Strength,* and *Nutrition and Strength.*

Bob Hoffman, the next pioneer in American weight training and bodybuilding, bought Mac-Fadden's *Strength* magazine in the early 1930s, changing its name to *Strength & Health.* That magazine has been continuously published to this day.

While Hoffman performed yeoman work publicizing weight training for promoting fitness, improving physical appearance, improving athletic performance, and as competitive bodybuilding, he was primarily interested in competitive weight lifting. Bob Hoffman was, in fact, chosen several times as the Olympic coach for weight lifting.

With Bob Hoffman diverted mainly by competitive weight lifting, it fell to an entrepreneur named Joe Weider to do the main work in promoting weight training for competitive bodybuilding and for improved health and physical appearance. Joe Weider—along with his wife, Betty—is also largely responsible for ultimately having weight training accepted by women as an ideal exercise medium.

Joe Weider began publishing *Your Physique* magazine in 1940. The magazine underwent several title changes over the years, but it has been continuously published. Today it is called *Muscle & Fitness* and is literally the Bible of weight training and bodybuilding worldwide. *Muscle & Fitness* has an international circulation of more than one million readers, half of them in America.

In the late 1940s, Joe Weider and his brother, Ben, founded the International Federation of Bodybuilders (IFBB), which now has a membership of 116 national federations, making bodybuilding the seventh most popular sport internationally. Due to the efforts of the Weider brothers, bodybuilding is on the verge of being accepted into the Olympic Games. And through

their efforts, numerous professional bodybuilders—ourselves included—are able to make handsome livings from the sport.

Weight training for athletes was abhorred by coaches in the late 1950s and early 1960s. Ultimately, sports coaches came to realize that stronger athletes are better athletes. Today, almost all athletes—male and female—in virtually every imaginable sport are encouraged to train with weights.

Clearly, weight training for all purposes has come of age!

HOW IT WORKS

The human body has a remarkable ability to adapt to stress. If it is forced to run for long periods of time, the body improves the endurance of its skeletal muscles, the efficiency of its heart and vascular system, and the volume and efficiency of its lungs.

In the same manner, if the body is forced to lift a heavy weight periodically, its muscles adapt in size, strength, and physiological efficiency to be able to comfortably lift the load. This concept is known as *muscle overloading.* If a muscle is progressively overloaded day by day, it is forced to keep growing in size and strength. This progressive overloading of a muscle is the heart and soul of weight training and bodybuilding.

Physiologically, it was once thought that an overload caused muscle fibers to break down under stress and then rebuild themselves larger and stronger during periods of rest. Modern physiologists, however, have disproven this theory. Instead, they say that muscle growth (which is scientifically called *muscle hypertrophy*) is caused by inhibition of catabolism in individual muscle cells.

We are sure that very few readers will have the remotest understanding of "inhibition of catabolism," so we shall briefly explain this concept. In all muscle tissue (indeed, in all tissues of the body) there are two types of metabolism (energy and matter transfer). One type of metabolism is called *anabolism,* which refers to a building up of tissue. The other type of metabolism is called *catabolism,* which is the breaking down of tissue.

In most human bodies, there is an equilibrium (balance) between anabolism and catabolism in the muscles. Muscle cells are broken

your physique

MARCH /30c

A Magazine For Men Who
Want To Improve Their Bodies

LEO ROBERT

AMERICA'S MOST MUSCULAR MAN
arms 17.5", chest 46", thighs 24"
Photo by Warner

Cover of March 1951 issue of Joe Weider's classic magazine, *Your Physique* (the forerunner of *Muscle & Fitness*).

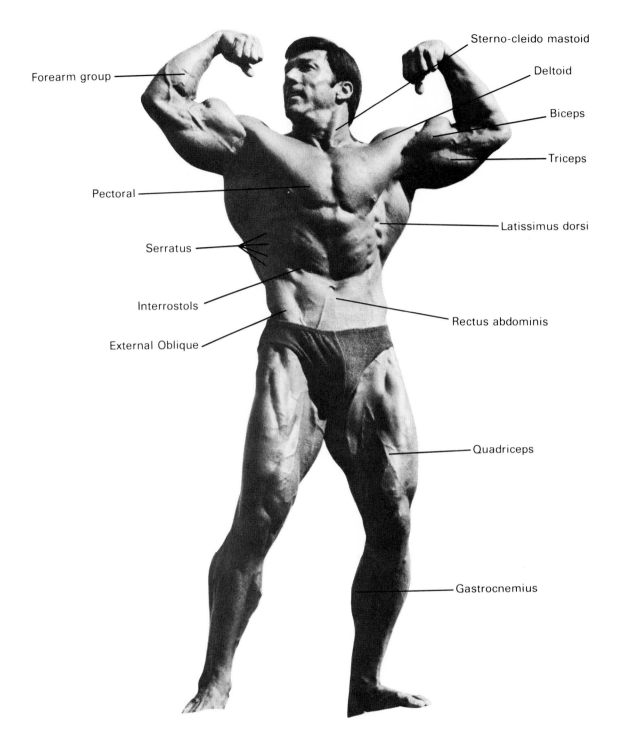

Forearm group

Pectoral

Serratus

Interrostols

External Oblique

Sterno-cleido mastoid

Deltoid

Biceps

Triceps

Latissimus dorsi

Rectus abdominis

Quadriceps

Gastrocnemius

SURFACE ANATOMY—FRONT

down at the same rate as others are being created, so the muscles stay at a constant mass and strength.

Classically, it was thought that weight training stimulated anabolism of muscle tissue, which caused the body's skeletal muscles to hypertrophy and grow stronger. Now, however, we know that resistance exercise inhibits (or reduces the rate of) catabolism. When the rate of anabolism remains constant and the catabolic rate is reduced, the net effect is a relatively higher rate of anabolism. And *that* is what

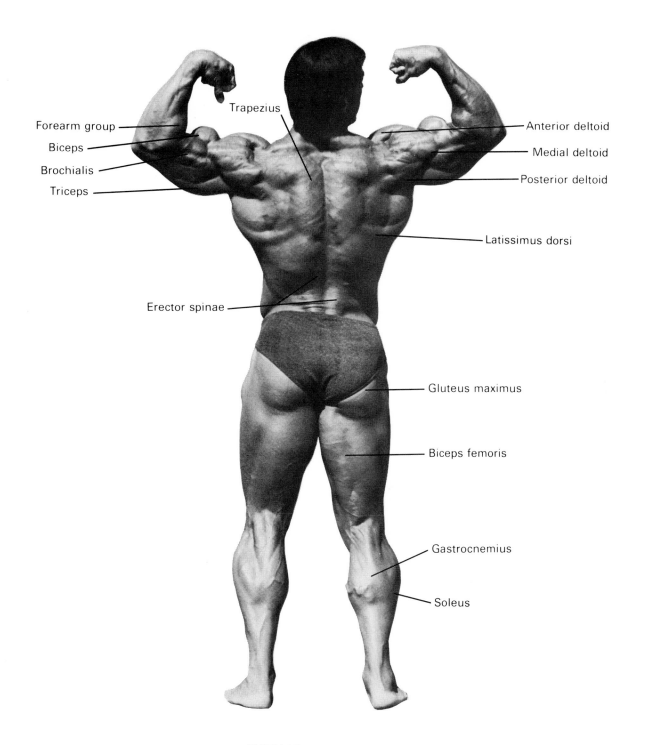

Forearm group

Biceps

Brochialis

Triceps

Trapezius

Anterior deltoid

Medial deltoid

Posterior deltoid

Latissimus dorsi

Erector spinae

Gluteus maximus

Biceps femoris

Gastrocnemius

Soleus

SURFACE ANATOMY—BACK

causes a muscle to grow in size and strength when you train it with progressively heavier weights.

This physiological process is universal in human beings. It works the same for everyone, although the muscles of various individuals re-spond to an overload stress at varying rates of speed and to various ultimate degrees. Younger individuals, for example, will find their muscles growing in size and strength more quickly than will men and women in their 60s and 70s. And men, because their male hormones are more conducive to muscle hypertrophy, will find that their bodies respond much more quickly and to a far greater degree to weight training than will women. We will discuss the differences between male and female weight trainers in much greater detail later in this chapter.

MUSCLE MYTHS

Since weight training has come out of the closet only during the last decade, there are still numerous myths associated with the activity. We are sure that at some point most readers have heard that weight training will make you muscle bound, will stunt your growth, or will make women look like men. As a result, we will now discuss the six most common myths about weight training, plus the truth behind each of these popular misconceptions.

1. *Weight training will make you muscle bound.* On the contrary, regular weight training actually improves muscle and joint flexibility. This has been proven in numerous scientific studies dating back to the early 1950s. Even hugely muscled champion male bodybuilders are far more flexible than sedentary individuals.

Despite his huge muscle size, Boyer is quite flexible.

2. *Weight training will make a woman look like a man.* Even the most cursory glance at Val's photos throughout this book will reveal that she still appears classically feminine, even after years of weight training. Later in this chapter we will discuss in detail why weight training cannot make a woman look like a man, but for now suffice to say that a woman's natural hormonal balance will prevent her from developing large, clearly delineated, masculine appearing muscles. Added muscle tissue merely appears as new and feminine curves on a woman's body.

3. *Weight training will slow you down.* This statement is patently absurd, because most athletes utilize weight workouts as a supplement to training for their sport. And they use weight training specifically to improve their speed. While reaction time (the speed with which your mind can receive a visual, aural, or tactile stimulus; interpret it; and cause a muscle to begin to contract) is an inherited quality that can't be improved, there is a scientifically proven relationship between muscle strength and actual speed of movement. The stronger the thigh and calf muscles of a sprinter, for example, the faster he or she will be able to run.

4. *Weight training will wreck your back, knees, and other joints.* This will never happen to you as long as you faithfully follow the warm-up procedures outlined in this book, pay strict attention to recommended safety practices, and maintain the correct biomechanical (body) positionings described for each exercise. Both of us have suffered muscle and joint injuries participating in other sports, but we have never incurred injuries of any sort while weight training or bodybuilding.

5. *Your muscles will turn to fat as soon as you stop weight training.* To begin with, it is physiologically impossible for muscle to turn to fat. When an overload stress is no longer regularly placed on a muscle, the muscle will gradually atrophy (shrink in size), until it has returned to nearly its original size. Even if you never again touch a weight, the muscle will always remain a little larger and stronger than it was when you started weight training, however. In general, a muscle will atrophy at about the same rate it reached its ultimate degree of hypertrophy. In other words, if it took you a year

to build yourself up, it will take about a year for your body to return to its original state.

It *is* possible to gain body fat after ceasing weight training or bodybuilding—or any other form of exercise that burns up calories, for that matter—if a former athlete's diet is not adjusted to compensate for the calories no longer being burned off in training sessions. With a slight reduction in daily caloric intake, however, you will never get fat if you quit weight training. And besides, 95% of all men and women who survive their first three months of weight training are hooked for life and will never stop their weight workouts short of a major injury, severe illness, or death!

6. *Weight training will stunt your growth.* Since a large percentage of men and women take up weight training during adolescence, this is a common fear among parents. The fear is fueled by the fact that very few top-level competitive male bodybuilders (save the 6'5" Lou Ferrigno) are taller than 5'8" or 5'9" in height. In actuality, competitive bodybuilders are slightly shorter than average because of a sort of sports Darwinism. Essentially, they are *naturally selected,* because it's easier to fill out a 5'8" body with huge muscles than it is to do so for a 7'2" body. Additionally, mesomorphic men (those who are naturally husky and muscular) tend to be of average—or slightly less than average—height, and mesomorphs make the best bodybuilders.

Scientific research has demonstrated that regular exercise and a diet that is nutritionally healthy (two of the most basic tenets of weight training and bodybuilding) will result in a significant average increase in height for both men and women. So, if anything, weight training will *stimulate* rather than stunt your growth.

DISADVANTAGES OF WEIGHT TRAINING

Despite the fact that we are personally sold on the values of weight training, we must admit that there are three disadvantages to the activity. Happily, however, there are valid antidotes to each of these disadvantages. Noting the best method to counteract each one, we will now discuss the three disadvantages of weight training.

1. *Weight training is boring.* Because of its inherently repetitive nature, weight training can be boring, particularly if the same exercises and training programs are followed for long periods of time. There are, however, literally hundreds of weight training exercises in existence for each muscle group. And with over a thousand weight training exercises to draw from, you can create an infinite variety of training programs, which effectively prevents boredom. In this book we have space to present only a few more than 50 exercises with variations on each bringing the total to approximately 100. Even so, with 100 exercises you could formulate a different training program for every day of the year!

2. *Weight training builds less cardiorespiratory fitness than other physical activities.* Indeed, weight training is intended primarily to build strength, so when used in a normal fashion it develops less heart-lung endurance than running, cycling, swimming, and other aerobic activities. With a specialized type of weight training called *circuit training* (discussed in detail in Chapter 5), however, it is possible to achieve an aerobic effect with weights very comparable to that achieved through running. And with circuit training you can develop superior overall muscle strength at the same time you are building a high degree of cardiorespiratory fitness. This has led some physical fitness experts to state that circuit training with weights is the best all-around physical fitness activity.

3. *All men and women will inevitably gain some muscle weight through weight training.* Even though this is actually a benefit when added body weight is in the form of functional muscle tissue, many men and women live in mortal fear of gaining even an ounce of body weight. As you gain a few ounces or a few pounds of muscular body weight, you will undoubtedly be improving your physical appearance because muscle tissue is more dense than fat tissue, and muscle therefore weighs more than fat. We are sure that virtually anyone will agree that a lean and firm looking man or woman is far more physically attractive than an obese individual.

ADVANTAGES OF WEIGHT TRAINING

Of course we are somewhat biased in saying

this, but the advantages of weight training and bodybuilding far outweigh the disadvantages of these activities. And as we have already demonstrated, the disadvantages of weight training can be virtually eliminated if the correct training and attitudinal strategies are followed.

There are four primary advantages of weight training that make this activity far superior to most other forms of exercise. Let's discuss each of these advantages in detail.

1. *Weight training allows selectivity in stressing individual muscles.* As we mentioned earlier, there are hundreds of weight training exercises for each skeletal muscle in the human body. There are even numerous exercises that will stress a small segment of a muscle group (such as the posterior third of the deltoid, or shoulder, muscle) in relative isolation from the rest of the muscle group. Because of the selectivity of weight training, you can use barbells, dumb-

Boyer squats with 315 pounds while Val does dumbbell curls with only 10 pounds in each hand.

bells, and resistance training machines to exercise your entire body, or just a small part of your body, something impossible with other forms of physical activity.

The ability you have of choosing exercises to zero in on single muscle groups makes weight training an ideal exercise technique for rehabilitating injuries. If, for example, a baseball or softball player has pulled a hamstring muscle, the muscle at the back of his or her injured thigh will be relatively weak once it has healed.

Through the use of leg curls—an exercise that isolates stress on the hamstring muscles—the injured muscle can be quickly rehabilitated to its original strength level. If an athlete desires to do so, he or she can actually make an injured muscle *much* stronger than it was prior to being injured.

2. *Weight training allows a range of resistance that is virtually unlimited.* With gymnastics and calisthenics, a man or woman must use a portion or all of his or her body weight to provide resistance in an exercise. Often, a person is simply too weak to do exercises that depend so much on body weight. On the other end of the scale, a gymnast or calisthenics enthusiast can never progress to using more than his or her body weight in an exercise movement. Therefore, the development of strength and muscle mass is limited to what can be produced by exercises using an individual's body weight.

With weight training, however, as little as one pound can be used in each hand for a variety of exercises. We have worked in rehabilitating numerous geriatric patients, all of whom have been able to handle one pound in each hand for virtually any exercise. On the other end of the scale, competitive powerlifters handle mind-boggling weights. Men have done squats (a deep knee bend movement) with more than 900 pounds loaded on a barbell and balanced across their shoulders. Women have done the same movement with over 500 pounds. Obviously, no other form of exercise allows the use of resistance ranging from 1–2 pounds to nearly 1000 pounds!

3. *In combination with diet, weight training makes it easy to normalize body weight.* The number of significantly overweight Americans approaches 40% of our total population. And there are also hundreds of thousands of seriously underweight men and women in our country. Exact methods for using weight training and diet to gain or lose weight are discussed in Chapter 4. For now, suffice to say that by combining specialized diet with specific weight training programs, you can either gain or lose body weight with relative ease until you have reached a normal weight. No other type of exercise will accomplish both of these functions when combined with healthy nutritional practices as efficiently as weight training.

4. *Weight training results in very fast strength*

gains. No physical activity will increase muscular strength as quickly as weight training will or to the ultimate degree that is possible through weight training. An average beginning male weight trainee can increase the strength of all of his muscle groups by at least 30% in one month of training, while an average woman can increase her beginning strength levels by at least 20%. Some highly motivated men have doubled their strength in only 6–8 weeks of steady weight training.

MEN'S vs. WOMEN'S WEIGHT TRAINING

Since this book is intended for use by men and by women, it's important to know the similarities and differences between how men and women train with weights. Generally speaking, there are a preponderance of similarities and only a few minor differences in how men and women weight train. This has not been what men and women have thought in the past.

Traditionally, men and women were supposed to be entirely different creatures, and as such required radically different approaches to weight training and other forms of exercise. At one point, for example, the longest Olympic Games footrace for women was 800 meters (approximately a half mile) in length, while the longest men's race was the marathon (26 miles, 385 yards). This was the situation because women were thought (by men) to be too frail to withstand the rigors of longer races, or the rigors of a "man's" weight workout. Today, thousands of women have run marathons in less than three hours and the women's world record is only a little more than 15 minutes slower than the men's record.

In weight training and bodybuilding, men were expected to do long, intense, heavy resistance workouts, with exercises done for each muscle group. This was intended to build great strength and large muscles. Women, in contrast, were traditionally limited to using very light weights, doing short workouts, and directing exercises to only selected body areas (usually the thighs, hips, buttocks, abdomen, and bustline). Back and arm training were to be avoided at all cost!

Today, women train every bit as hard as do their male counterparts. Women have greater endurance than men and can endure longer workouts, but they are generally much less powerful than men.

Men and women can and do train together using identical workouts, *if* they wish to train equally hard and can schedule a time when they are able to train together. We often do our workouts together, particularly when preparing for the World Couples' Bodybuilding Championships or a dual posing exhibition. It's an enjoyable way for any couple to spend time together.

There is much good to be said about male-female training partnerships, because the physical differences of each partner tend to complement those of the other. Women, with their greater endurance, can pull a male partner through a longer and faster workout than he would normally be able to take on his own. And men, with their greater strength, tend to force their female partners to train with much heavier-than-normal poundages.

Val demonstrates that a woman can train with heavy weights, but a woman's hormonal secretions won't allow her to work out as heavily as a man.

Practically speaking, however, few couples actually train together on identical workout programs. Often the husband or boyfriend is training super intensely for sports or bodybuilding competition, while the wife or girlfriend has no greater goal than to firm up and lose or gain a couple of pounds. In this type of situation it's still enjoyable for both to work out at the same time, since this offers the harder training person moral support and gives a couple one more enjoyable activity that they can do together. This is how it often works for us, because I compete so frequently throughout the year and Val is usually more concerned about using weight workouts to maintain her figure.

Earlier we hinted that there are physiological differences between men and women. The main physiological difference is in hormonal balances. Both men and women secrete *testosterone* (the male sex hormone responsible for male secondary sex characteristics like deep voice, large and strong muscles, and facial hair growth) and *estrogen* (the female sex hormone responsible for such female secondary sex characteristics as breast development, a wider pelvic structure, and smaller, weaker muscles). Although both sexes secrete each hormone, men produce more testosterone than estrogen, which gives them far more muscle mass and much greater strength than women. Females, in contrast, primarily secrete estrogen, which drastically limits the degree of muscle mass and physical strength that they can develop. Estrogen also causes any muscle tissue that a woman does build to appear on her body as soft, feminine curves.

Because of the hormonal balance differences between the sexes, men will always be dramatically stronger than women in performing any weight training exercise. And because their skeletal structures are equally thick throughout their bodies, men tend to have a unique balance between upper body and lower body strength. We can call this type of strength balance *normal*. Women, in contrast, are anatomically heavier in their lower body skeletal and muscular structures than they are in their upper bodies. Therefore, women tend to be much weaker than men in their upper bodies than they are by comparison in their legs.

Physiologically, women tend to have more

endurance and higher pain thresholds than men. Some experts say that these differences are Nature's endowment to women that makes car-

Weight training will only make the differences between men and women more dramatic.

rying and giving birth to children easier for them to endure. Practically speaking, greater endurance and a superior ability to accept pain allow a woman to balance out a man's inherently superior strength. Thus, when a man and a woman decide to become training partners, their physiological strengths and weaknesses balance out.

FAMILY WEIGHT TRAINING

As easily as weight training can be an activity for couples, it can be adapted to serve as a family recreational pursuit as well. Obviously, children should never be subjected to an adult's high intensity workouts, but if they show an interest in "being like Mommy and Daddy," there's no reason why they can't be given light workouts to be done along with yours.

Valerie and I have seen children as young as two or three years of age mimicking their parents in weight workouts. It's good exercise for them, although their juvenile hormonal balances won't allow them to build any muscle mass or appreciable strength until they reach puberty. As long as children are closely supervised, however, there will be no danger to them while they are enjoying their workouts.

It is vital that you give your child correct training information in terms that he or she can comprehend. It's especially important that you constantly monitor their biomechanical position for each exercise. Of course, you should always endeavor to present a flawless example of a competent weight trainer to children.

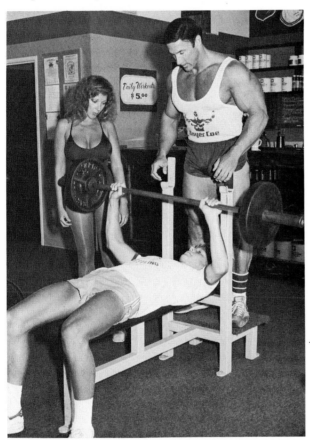

Val and Boyer don't have children yet, but they share the spirit of family workouts with youngsters in the gym.

Bear in mind that young children have very short attention spans and that their attention spans and ability to concentrate will improve slowly as they mature. Therefore, don't be surprised if your son or daughter is playing with the weights one moment and with the cat the next. Just be patient, let your son or daughter set his or her own pace, and try to make your child's workouts fun.

WHAT'S NEXT?

Chapter 2 will include a lengthy discussion of basic training information. To safely undertake your first weight workout it will be necessary to familiarize yourself thoroughly with all of the basic information in Chapter 2.

Looking farther ahead, Chapter 3 is devoted to detailed descriptions with clear performance illustrations of more than 50 weight training exercises, most of which you will use for as long as you train with weights.

Chapter 4 presents a variety of weight training programs for beginning, intermediate, and advanced weight trainees. It also includes sample menus and nutrition principles for losing weight while weight training.

Chapter 5 is devoted to advanced training techniques, primarily in relation to competitive bodybuilding. In addition to discussing advanced training secrets, we will thoroughly explore competitive bodybuilding nutritional philosophies and the controversial use of bodybuilding drugs. It also includes a detailed summary of our exact precompetition training programs.

At the back of the book we have included a short glossary of common weight training and bodybuilding terms for quick reference if you run across an expression you don't understand in the text of this book.

Boyer and Val pose for a painting by Jim Zar.

2
Basic Training Tips

I can vividly recall being pinned under a heavy barbell while bench pressing just a few weeks after I started training. Fortunately, the barbell landed on my chest instead of my neck. But there were still two or three anxious minutes before mooselike bellows for help brought my parents out to the garage to rescue me.

It is absolutely essential for your own safety that you thoroughly master all of the information set forth in this chapter before you even set foot in a gym or weight room. If you try working out without the proper indoctrination—as contained in this chapter—you could seriously injure yourself. And if you ignore the safety instructions toward the end of this chapter, you actually could kill yourself while lifting weights.

PHYSICAL EXAMINATIONS

Any man or woman over 30 years of age—especially if he or she has led a sedentary life for a year or more—should have a physician's physical examination before starting *any* exercise program. For men and women over 40 years of age, this physical exam should also include a stress test electrocardiogram (EKG).

A competent physician can accurately assess your relative degree of physical condition as well as the amount and intensity of exercise that you can initially handle. The intensity progressions we present in this book may be deemed by your doctor to be too strenuous for you. If so, *always* follow your physician's instructions. He knows you and your physical capabilities far more intimately than we do.

FUNDAMENTAL DEFINITIONS

There is a glossary of weight training and bodybuilding terms at the back of this book. You can refer to that glossary whenever you encounter a term you don't understand. There are, however, several basic definitions germaine to weight training that you must master in order to understand much of the information following in this chapter and in Chapter 3.

Weight training is a form of exercise using barbells, dumbbells, and resistance machines to accomplish any of several physical improvement goals.

Bodybuilding is one subdivision of weight training in which weights are used to reshape your body. Bodybuilding can also be a competitive sport. The term *bodysculpture* is occasionally used interchangeably with bodybuilding, and it is a term most frequently used in a feminine context.

Weight lifting is another competitive form of weight training in which competitors try to outdo each other in the amount of weight they can lift. Weight lifting for men and women is subdivided into *Olympic lifting* (the form of weight lifting contested in the Olympic Games) and *powerlifting*. Olympic lifting consists of two lifts (the snatch, and the clean and jerk), whereas powerlifting is comprised of three lifts (the squat, bench press, and deadlift).

Boyer demonstrates his form of a clean and jerk, one of two competitive Olympic lifts.

An *exercise,* also called a *movement,* is the actual physical maneuver done with resistance equipment to develop a part of the body. A deep knee bend, for example, is a calisthenics exercise, while a barbell squat is the equivalent weight training exercise. *Exercise* can also be used as a verb, as in "to exercise," "to work out," or "to train."

A *repetition* (frequently abbreviated to *rep*) is each full and complete cycle of an exercise. In a deep knee bend, one repetition would be the complete movement cycle starting with the legs held completely straight, then with the legs fully bent, and finally, fully straightened again. Ordinarily, series of reps are done of each exercise, with little or no pause between consecutive repetitions.

A *set* is a distinct group of repetitions. As an example, if you did 20 consecutive reps of a deep knee bend and then stopped exercising, you would have completed one set of 20 reps in this movement. Multiple sets are usually done of each exercise with a *rest interval* of 60 seconds or so between sets.

A *routine* (alternately called a *training program, program, workout,* or *training schedule*) is the total of all sets of each exercise done on a particular training day. Usually, the same routine is repeated two or three times per week.

THE EQUIPMENT YOU WILL USE

A barbell is the most basic piece of weight training equipment. We have provided a labeled photo to acquaint you with the name of each part of a barbell.

There are two basic types of barbells, an *exercise barbell* and an *Olympic barbell*. Olympic bars are specialized and sophisticated apparati used in competitive weight lifting and in workouts for exercises in which you might use extremely heavy weights. Olympic bars are 6½ to 7 feet in length, and the part of the bar on which the plates fit will be significantly thicker than the handle of the barbell. Olympic bars are constructed so the handle rotates smoothly and easily. An empty Olympic bar weighs 45 pounds (20 kilograms [kg.] internationally) and each of its collars weighs five pounds (2½ kg.).

Exercise barbells are most commonly five feet in length, although a few are four feet and some six feet long. With collars in place, exercise bars weigh approximately five pounds per foot. The weight of this bar—as well as that of an Olympic bar—must be taken into account when assembling the correct workout weight for a particular exercise.

A barbell, with parts labeled, on a squat rack.

The *bar* of an exercise barbell is usually an inch in diameter. Ordinarily a hollow metal tube called a *sleeve* is fitted over this bar to allow the barbell to rotate more easily in your hands (although still far less easily than an Olympic bar rotates). If a sleeve doesn't rotate at all, use a lightweight oil to coat the bar before replacing the sleeve.

The sleeve of an exercise barbell, or the handle of an Olympic bar, is grooved with *knurlings*. These cross-hatched grooves make it easier to grip the bar of the barbell when your hands

Seated calf machine.

are sweaty, as they often are during a weight training workout.

Inside collars are either welded in place or locked into position with *set screws* threaded through the collars and tightened against the bar. These collars keep the *plates* (flat metal or vinyl-covered, concrete discs) from sliding inward and injuring your hands during an exercise. These plates come in a wide range of poundages, from as little as 1¼ pounds to as much as 100 pounds each.

Metal plates are preferable in most cases to the vinyl-covered version. They are far more durable and you can load a much heavier poundage on a barbell with metal plates than with the bulkier vinyl-concrete plates. If you work out at home, however, the vinyl-covered plates are easier on floors.

Plates are secured in place on the bar with *outside collars,* which again are screwed to the bar by tightening down set screws. The set screws of outside collars usually include a handle arrangement of some sort to allow these collars to be quickly and easily tightened and loosened by hand. In contrast, inside collars are seldom moved from one position to the next, so their set screws are usually tightened with a wrench.

In organized gyms and health spas, you will find series barbells and dumbbells called *fixed weights,* which have various poundages perma-

Leg extension machine.

nently welded into place. These fixed barbells are graduated in five- or ten-pound increments (the weight on the bar is usually painted on its plates for easy identification). Fixed barbells and dumbbells are normally stored on racks around the gym. Whenever you use one of these weights, it is good etiquette (and a good safety practice) to return the weight to its proper rack when finished with it.

The obvious advantage of using fixed weights is that you can avoid the time-consuming procedure of having to constantly change weights on an adjustable barbell set. When you're trying to stay warm during a workout by taking short rest intervals between sets, changing the weights on an adjustable barbell set can defeat your purpose.

Dumbbells are short versions of barbells, usually 12–15 inches in length. They are intended to be used with one hand, or most commonly with one in each hand. Other than the length, dumbbells have all of the terminology and characteristics of barbells.

Seated pressing machine.

There are numerous other pieces of free-weight apparatus commonly used in gyms and health spas across America. These apparati include numerous types of *benches, weight support racks, pulleys, chinning bars, dipping bars,* and a variety of *leg machines.* The use of each of these pieces of equipment will become easily understandable once you read all of the exercise descriptions in Chapter 3.

Universal Gym machines are frequently found in gyms and spas. They offer the utility of apparati to exercise every body part contained in a single exercise unit. Most school weight rooms around America will have a Universal Gym, because up to 10 trainees can exercise on one simultaneously. The machines cost in the range of $2000–$3000. That expense is a good investment for institutions like schools and YMCAs in which groups of men and women will need to train at one time, but extremely excessive for a home gym!

Nautilus machines began to gain popularity during the late 1960s, and now they are in widespread use across America, particularly in health clubs called Nautilus Fitness Centers, which offer memberships for $300 or more per year. It would be difficult for most private citizens to train on Nautilus machines in their garages or basements, since it requires an installation of 10–12 machines to work the full body. Each machine costs between $2500 and $5000.

Overall, Nautilus machines provide a superior form of resistance on each muscle group, since they place an equally balanced force on the muscle along the full range of movement for

Nautilus abdominal machine.

each exercise. Free weights and most other machines don't offer such balanced resistance.

On the other side of the coin, however, there are only two or three movements that can be done on Nautilus machines for each muscle group. This lack of variety can be a drawback in both Nautilus and Universal Gym machines, because it can lead to boredom. With free weights, in contrast, you can do literally 100 or more distinctly different exercises for each body part. As a result, we feel that both Nautilus and Universal Gym machines—as well as all other exercise machines—are most effectively used in conjunction with barbells, dumbbells, and other free-weight apparati.

Resistance training machines do offer one advantage over free weights, however. Although the danger of being pinned under a barbell and injured is virtually nonexistent if the safety procedures outlined later in this chapter are followed, some inexperienced or poorly instructed trainees have been injured and even killed lifting free weights. All exercise machines obviate this risk, because they are constructed so no resistance is on the body if a trainee fails to complete a full repetition of any exercise.

Overall, the least expensive and most utilitarian weight training equipment consists of an adjustable barbell-and-dumbbell set. A 150-pound set will be adequate for starters and costs only about $50–$70. Later, such a set can be upgraded simply by purchasing additional metal plates—either new or used—to provide even greater resistance for each of your exercises.

If the cost of a new barbell set seems a bit steep to you, try buying one at a neighborhood garage sale. You can probably acquire one in that manner for only about 25% of the cost of a new set. Remember, whether you buy a new or used set, you're paying a one-time fee. If you were a gym or health spa member, your dues would be paid each year, not on a one-time basis.

MENTAL FACTORS

There are several mental tricks that you can use to improve the quality of your weight training and bodybuilding workouts. It's been said that the mind is the strongest "muscle" in the human body. This is true because the brain is the organ that controls all of the skeletal muscles, as well as other voluntary and involuntary functions in the human body. Properly used, your mind can greatly improve the quality of your training, particularly if you are a competitive bodybuilder.*

The first mental training technique you should use—particularly at the beginning level of training—is to mentally *track* each exercise in your mind before actually doing it. And you should use this mental tracking procedure on each new exercise until you have completely mastered the movement. Tracking simply amounts to imagining the exercise as it is correctly performed for a few repetitions. Pay particular attention to using precise biomechanical positions for each exercise as it is described and illustrated in Chapter 3. Mental tracking will improve your body coordination in each exercise and will help prevent you from assuming biomechanical positions that might leave you open to injury.

Second, you should mentally concentrate on every repetition of each set of all of the exercises you do in your training routine. Bodybuilders talk about "getting the mind into it," which means concentrating fully on feeling the muscle(s) affected by each exercise as they are moving and working under full resistance. In essence, a strong link can be developed between the mind and the working muscles. And once this link has reached full strength it can drastically improve the quality of your workouts, as well as the degree of results you can expect from your training.

To learn how to correctly concentrate when training, begin by simply thinking about the muscle(s) being worked by an exercise as you are doing that movement. In Chapter 3 we clearly identify which muscles are stressed by each exercise. Feel the correct muscles contracting and extending under the weight load you are putting on them, and *feel* them getting progressively more fatigued with each successive repetition of a movement.

With time, you will gradually become increasingly adept at concentrating strictly on the mus-

*See the section on "Visualization" in Chapter 5 for detailed information on how champion bodybuilders positively program their minds for success.

Concentrate deeply before doing a heavy set.

cle groups you are training, until you have reached a point where you can completely shut out all external distractions. Champion bodybuilders become so adept at concentrating on an exercise and the muscles it works that you could burn the gym down around them during a set and they probably wouldn't even notice the flames!

A third mental technique that you'll find useful in weight training and bodybuilding—or in any other sport—is goal setting. Properly chosen goals can give you a road map to success, which allows you to choose an expressway to the top rather than a winding, country road to nowhere. No athlete we have ever known has been successful at his or her sport without setting attainable goals, systematically reaching them, and then setting higher goals.

There are three types of goals that you should set—ultimate goals, long-range goals, and short-term goals. The ancient Chinese philosopher, Confucius, had a good grasp of goal setting when he observed that, "The journey of a thou-sand miles is started with a single step." In the paradigm, we can define the 1000-mile journey as an ultimate goal and each individual step, from first to last, along that 1000-mile walk as a short-range goal. The way stations at which we stop to rest each night are long-range goals.

Ultimate goals should be set as high as the level of excellence you can reasonably expect to achieve with a lifetime of proper and consistent training, good diet, long-range mental conditioning, and good luck. Typical ultimate goals include becoming an Olympic or World Champion in a sport, setting a world record, gaining or losing 50–100 pounds and achieving the physical appearance you desire, or attaining optimum health and physical fitness. Ultimate goals are the big "pie in the sky" that you will strive diligently for years to reach. Ultimate goals also are so mind-boggling in magnitude that they seem virtually impossible to reach. Can you, for example, conceive of walking 1000 miles? Probably not, although you may well walk much farther in a lifetime of short strolls and not even know it.

To put ultimate goals into perspective, it is best to set yearly *long-range goals* of smaller magnitude. Perhaps you can set a long-range goal of walking 100 miles, which is more easily conceptualized than walking 1000 miles. Still, 10 years of reaching 100-mile walking goals definitely equals an ultimate goal of walking 1000 miles.

Short-range goals are of even a smaller scale, such as each step along a 1000-mile journey. Perhaps you have set a goal of gaining 10 pounds of muscular body weight in a year, or one of improving your bench press workout poundage by 50 pounds. These long-range goals are far more easily attained if you shoot for monthly short-range goals of gaining one pound of muscle or adding five pounds to your bench press. If you reached such short-range goals each month for a year, you would actually have exceeded your long-range goals for that year.

Goal setting, then, gives a focus to your weight training and bodybuilding. Without such targets at which to aim and hit, you will not progress very quickly in your training. So, take time now to set your ultimate, long-range, and short-range goals. Write them down in your training diary and then go for your goals!

The fourth mental technique you should use is an old one, but still a valid one: *the power of positive thinking.* You must be positive in your approach to your weight training and toward reaching your goals, or you can never hope to be successful in this activity, or even in life itself.

Successful men and women in all walks of life—not just athletics—*never* consider the possibility that they might fail. Occasionally they do fail to reach a goal, and they admit to that failure, but they still never allow negative thoughts to enter their minds. Follow the examples of successful individuals and always attempt to keep a positive attitude toward your training and toward life in general. Be positive and you *will* be successful.

Finally, we have found that virtually everyone has difficulty maintaining 100% mental intensity for an entire one- or two-hour workout. This is nothing to be ashamed of, because the mental involvement of anyone really into weight training or bodybuilding is like a *sine* wave pattern, with peak intensity only while a set of an exercise is actually being performed. So after a set has been completed, you should relax your mind and body for 30–40 seconds and then begin to gear up mentally for the next set, peaking your concentration again for that set.

WHERE TO TRAIN

There are five basic places at which men and women weight train. These are: (1) at home; (2) in a high school or college weight room; (3) at a YMCA; (4) at a health spa or Nautilus facility; and (5) in a commercial bodybuilding gym. All five of these locations have advantages and disadvantages, but as we will demonstrate to you, a bodybuilding gym will be the best place to perform your workouts.

Many men and women begin weight training at home, because of the privacy and convenience home gym training affords. For many individuals—particularly women—it is embarrassing to train with weights in front of others, either because of clumsiness, lack of confidence, or poor physical appearance. You wouldn't be the first person to feel this way. For example, Lou Ferrigno, the champion bodybuilder who portrayed The Incredible Hulk on television for several years, was so painfully thin and shy that he trained with weights in his basement for several years before developing enough self-confidence to begin using a public gym.

Home gyms are also open for use 24 hours a day, while public weight training facilities have set hours for use. If you get the urge to work out at 3 a.m., it's far easier to do so at home than in a commercial gym, school weight room, or health spa, which may not be open again until 10 the next morning.

Two main disadvantages exist in home gym training. The first of these is lack of supervision and comradeship. When training alone, it's easy to get into bad exercise habits. And if you do heavy bench presses alone, you can even black out and/or have the weight fall across your neck and be strangled. With training partners, you will be more likely to maintain correct exercise form, you will not risk injury doing bench presses or other heavy movements, and you will have others with whom you can compare your progress.

The second disadvantage of home gym training is that it's usually impossible to equip a home gym as completely as a commercial gym will be equipped. Big gyms like Dan Howard's World Gym in Fountain Valley, California, where we train, have equipment installations valued into the hundreds of thousands of dollars. Still, with ingenuity and a little money, home gyms can be equipped sufficiently to permit excellent workouts with plenty of variety in them. And home gym equipment expenditures are a one-time investment, while gym and health spa dues must be paid yearly.

School and YMCA weight rooms vary widely in the quality and variety of equipment they contain. At a minimum, such exercise facilities might have a Universal Gym. A few are equipped as well as any commercial bodybuilding gym in America. Most fall somewhere in between these two extremes in the range of equipment they provide.

School weight rooms offer the advantage of being free for use by students, and YMCAs offer numerous other types of athletic facilities (basketball gyms, swimming pools, etc.) in addition to weight rooms. YMCA memberships vary in cost from city to city. At any rate, we suggest investigating all weight training facilities and gyms in your area—including taking a trial workout in each—before deciding on where to set up your weight training headquarters.

Health spas and Nautilus facilities usually are considered by their proprietors to be high-yield business enterprises, so membership fees can be quite high (in the range of $300–$500 per year, compared to $200–$225 per year at bodybuilding gyms). To most serious bodybuilders and weight trainers, the chrome-plated apparati at health spas are inadequate for hard training. Dumbbells seldom weigh more than a maximum of 65–70 pounds, which is laughably light to any male bodybuilder. Women's facilities at health spas usually are more poorly equipped than men's.

Since health spas cater to businessmen and their wives, who are interested in finding a shortcut to health, physical fitness, and improved appearance, anyone who trains hard with weights may be discriminated against in a spa. We know more than a few male and female bodybuilders who have been taken aside and firmly told, "Cool it! You're sweating so much that you're scaring away other customers." Still, spas provide a good social atmosphere for fitness-style weight workouts, so if improved appearance and fitness are your only goals, a health spa could be the perfect place for you to train.

Nautilus facilities have been established all over America, and they have become quite popular with the general public. Nautilus proponents claim that any man or woman can reach "optimum physical conditioning" in only 20 minutes of training three days a week on Nautilus machines, and this claim is attractive to the average person. "It's torture, but it works!" is the catchy slogan of one southern California chain of Nautilus training facilities. We wonder, however, how Nautilus boosters define "optimum physical conditioning." Obviously no male runner will receive enough endurance from one 20-minute circuit of training on Nautilus machines to run a mile in under four minutes. And no woman powerlifter will attain enough strength in such a short workout to be able to squat with over 400 pounds.

Several champion male bodybuilders—notably Mike Mentzer and Casey Viator—have been strong boosters of Nautilus machines and the Nautilus system of training. But while they train fewer total hours per week than most bodybuilders, Mentzer and Viator have had to train several times more than only one total hour a week to develop their massive and well-defined muscles.

Unfortunately, Nautilus facilities seldom have free weights on their premises, limiting their members to using only Nautilus machines. So they can accommodate a large clientele (and make more money), Nautilus proprietors usually require their members to enter a line of machines at a set point, then progress along this line sequentially. Since another member invariably will follow directly behind you, it becomes virtually impossible to do multiple sets of an exercise on any of the machines, should one of your muscle groups require more exercise than the rest of your body. For average strength development and improved appearance, however, Nautilus gyms are a viable alternative.

Far and away, the best place for all men and women to train—whether they are seeking just mildly improved physical appearance, are trying to better their sports performance, are competitive weight lifters, or are champion bodybuilders—is at a commercial bodybuilding gym. These gyms charge reasonable fees and, invariably, are superbly equipped with free weights, various exercise apparati, Universal Gyms, and even Nautilus machines. And these gyms have large numbers of experienced men and women—who can give you quality training advice—working out in them. It was at such a gym that Val began weight training.

The leading bodybuilding gyms in America are establishments like Dan Howard's World Gym (Fountain Valley, CA), Joe Gold's World Gym (Santa Monica, CA), Gold's Gym (Venice, CA), Boyer Coe's Body Masters (Metairie, LA), Red Lerille's Gym (Lafayette, LA), and the Mid City Gym (New York City). There are, however, bodybuilding gyms in virtually every town in America. A comprehensive listing of such gyms is printed each month in *Muscle & Fitness* magazine, which is available on most newsstands. Or, you can look in the yellow pages of your phone book under "Gymnasiums" or "Health Clubs" for listings of gyms in your area.

If you have a choice between several places to train (as is the case in large cities like New York, Chicago, and Los Angeles), base your choice primarily on how comfortable you feel in a gym and how high a quality of workout you can get from it. It's always a good idea to try one or two workouts in each gym before deciding on one. And you may even decide to train in two or more gyms, as do many top male and female bodybuilders, since this procedure adds even more variety to your workouts than training in a single gymnasium.

WHEN TO TRAIN

The time of day at which you train is a matter of personal choice and individual circumstances. Some persons are morning people, while others are night people, which can dictate the time to train since workouts are best undertaken when energy levels are highest. Gym hours and job, school, and family commitments can also have a bearing on when you train.

When I was a college student and had already started my business career, I found myself so busy that I could only fit my workouts in at the ungodly hours of 3–5 a.m.; still, I made great progress in my training and won the Mr. Universe title!

While it makes little difference what time of the day or night you work out, it is a good idea to train at the same time each day. The body thrives on regularity, and when you train at the same hour each day, your body will soon adapt to such regular stress by peaking its energies for that daily time period. This also will give you better workouts than if you constantly vary the time of day at which you train.

WORKOUT FREQUENCY

After each weight training session, your body will require approximately 40–45 hours to fully recuperate and prepare itself for the next workout. During this time period, your circulatory system removes waste products (fatigue by-products like lactic acid and carbon dioxide) from the muscles, replacing them with new supplies of muscle fuel (in the form of *glycogen,* a blood and muscle sugar) and oxygen. The muscles also need 40–45 hours to grow a little in size and strength between workouts.

If at least one full day of rest is not taken between training days for each muscle group, your muscles—and to some extent the rest of your body—will fail to recuperate fully. Then you will often overtrain (become stale or burned out) and muscle growth and strength increase will stop. Overtraining is fully discussed in Chapter 5, but for our purposes at the beginning level of weight training you can avoid it entirely by taking a rest day between each workout day.

At the beginning and low-intermediate levels of weight training, you can easily work your entire body in one training session, since you won't need to do a very high number of sets for each muscle. In this case, it is best to train three nonconsecutive days a week. Because the system leaves weekends free for other recreational pursuits, most beginners work out with weights on Mondays, Wednesdays, and Fridays. Tuesdays, Thursdays, and Saturdays—or any other combination of three nonconsecutive training days each week—can also be used.

Eventually you will be doing such a high number of sets for your body that it will be difficult to do a full-body workout in one day. Then an intermediate bodybuilder uses a *split routine* (described in detail in Chapter 4), which involves dividing the body into halves and doing half of the body one day, half the next, and then resting the third day. On the fourth day the cycle repeats. Such split routines allow shorter, albeit more frequent, workouts. They are workable in a recuperation sense—can be used without overtraining—because a muscle group is still allowed at least a full day of rest between training sessions. One body part simply rests on the day another is being trained.

Three muscle groups (the abdominals, calves, and forearms) are exceptions to the every-other-day training rule. You will find that these three muscle groups will benefit from 4–6 workouts per week once you reach the high-intermediate and advanced training levels. Some competitive bodybuilders even receive superior developmental results in their midsections from training their abdominal muscles twice each day, seven days a week for short periods of time before competing.

TRAINING CONSISTENCY

Once you commit yourself fully to weight training, you must understand that consistency of effort and training regularity are the keys to achieving maximum results from your workouts. Merely going through the motions in a workout can result in only minimal improvement, if any, in strength development and muscle tone, while giving each exercise 100% of your mental and physical energies each workout guarantees that you will gain strength, muscle tone, and muscle mass at an optimum rate.

Unless you are so ill that you must remain in bed, you should never miss a scheduled workout. One missed workout can set your progress back by as much as a week, because you will actually experience negative results from missing a training session. Therefore, it takes another workout just to bring yourself back up to the point where you were physically before missing a session, and a second workout to induce any new progress.

You also will find that one missed workout can easily lead to a second and a third, until you are no longer weight training at all. Therefore, you will make your greatest progress when you train consistently hard and with strict regularity.

Being fully involved with our marriage, business interests, and college classes, it was very easy for Val to rationalize missing a workout here and there. And she has done it. But it has only been when she disciplined herself to do every workout that she has made good progress physically.

All of what we have said in this section notwithstanding, you must recognize that your body undergoes natural, up-and-down energy cycles. Some days your 100% effort will fall far below that of other workout days, because your energy levels might be quite low. Energy fluctuates as a function of numerous factors, including amount and quality of sleep, diet, emotional stress, daily attitude changes, and what have been called biorhythmic cycles. Just ride out these energy lows and still give 100% to your training, and never use them as an excuse for missing a workout. An attitude like this will insure maximum results from your training.

PROGRESSION

As we mentioned in Chapter 1, muscles respond to an overload of resistance by growing larger and stronger. And if the muscles are progressively overloaded with greater and greater stress, they must continue to grow in size and strength. Therefore, *progression* of resistance overload is at the very heart of weight training and bodybuilding.

Physiologically, the body is lazy in adapting to stress of any sort, in that it only adapts sufficiently to accommodate the new stress level. If, for example, your body is normally capable of comfortably lifting a 50-pound sack of potatoes from the floor up to a table top, it will sense an overload when you lift a 55-pound sack of potatoes in the same manner. But the body will adapt to the 55-pound load by growing just strong enough to lift it comfortably. However, it won't under any circumstances adapt to lifting a 60-pound sack of potatoes *unless* it is subsequently forced to lift the 60-pound load.

In weight training, progression of overload can happen in three distinct ways, or in various combinations of these methods. The three ways weight trainers and bodybuilders progressively increase resistance are:

1. Increase the weight being used for a constant number of repetitions in an exercise.
2. Increase the number of repetitions done with a constant weight in an exercise.
3. Reduce the rest interval between sets of an exercise while maintaining a constant training weight, a constant number of sets of that exercise, and a constant number of repetitions for each set.

In most phases of weight training, both the exercise weight and the number of repetitions are progressively increased, one at a time in leapfrog fashion. Usually only champion competitive bodybuilders use decreased rest intervals between sets as a means of increasing training intensity (resistance), and then they ordinarily use this method for only a few weeks before competition.

For most weight training purposes, trainees will progressively increase resistance in each exercise by gradually increasing the number of repetitions done for an exercise until an *upper guide number* (usually 10–12 reps) has been reached. Then the training weight is increased by 5–10 pounds and the repetitions reduced to a *lower guide number* (usually 6–8 reps). The repetitions are again gradually increased to the upper guide number, the weight increased, and the reps reduced to the lower guide number again. Over a period of several years, such a repetition-and-weight progression can have both men and women using hundreds of pounds in some exercises.

To give you a better idea of what guide numbers are all about, turn briefly to Chapter 4 and glance at one of the numerous weight training workouts outlined therein. You will note that for each exercise a suggested range of repetitions is listed, e.g., "6–10 reps," or "8–12 reps." In these cases, "6" and "8" are the lower guide numbers, while "10" and "12" are the upper guide numbers for repetitions to be done each set.

To be very clear on how progression works, we will explain how to manipulate the reps and training poundages for a particular movement. Assuming that you can do eight repetitions with 40 pounds ("40 × 8" is a common way to abbreviate this weight–rep scheme) in the bench press and your suggested repetition range is "8–12," here is a chart listing one month of typical progression in this exercise:

	Monday	Wednesday	Friday
Week 1	40 × 8	40 × 9	40 × 10
Week 2	40 × 11	40 × 12	45 × 8
Week 3	45 × 9	45 × 10	45 × 11
Week 4	45 × 12	50 × 8	50 × 9, etc.

If you were used to doing 40 × 8 in the bench press, it would be quite a strain to suddenly be required to do 45 × 8. But there's very little difference in *feel* between doing 40 × 12 and 45 × 8, and it's relatively easy to increase your reps by one on every exercise each workout. Some days you'll be able to increase your reps by as many as two or three, while on a particularly bad day, you may not be able to increase your

repetitions at all. Overall, however, shoot for one extra rep—or a weight increase—on each exercise every workout.

We're often asked how much weight should be added to an exercise once the upper guide number for reps has been reached. For women, 5–10 pounds is usually an appropriate increase for leg and back exercises, while 2½–5 pounds will be about right for movements stressing the rest of the body. For men, these weight increases can be 10–20 pounds and 5–10 pounds respectively.

The foregoing example of progression was given for a single set of an exercise. Once past the first two to three weeks of training, however, you will do multiple sets (usually 3–5) of each exercise. In such a case, you should do all of the sets of an exercise before moving on to the next movement. You should also complete the upper guide number of reps for each set before increasing the training poundage for an exercise. Using our previous example, but modifying it for three sets of bench presses, here is a typical one-month progression in reps and weight:

	Monday	Wednesday	Friday
Week 1	50 × 8	50 × 10	50 × 11
	50 × 8	50 × 9	50 × 10
	50 × 8	50 × 8	50 × 10
Week 2	50 × 12	50 × 12	50 × 12
	50 × 11	50 × 12	50 × 12
	50 × 10	50 × 11	50 × 12
Week 3	55 × 8	55 × 10	55 × 11
	55 × 8	55 × 10	55 × 10
	55 × 8	55 × 9	55 × 10
Week 4	55 × 12	55 × 12	60 × 8
	55 × 11	55 × 12	60 × 8
	55 × 10	55 × 12	60 × 8, etc.

By following all of our suggestions for progressively increasing resistance for your exercises—as well as by training diligently and consistently—you will be assured of receiving optimum results from your weight training workouts, regardless of your goals.

REST INTERVALS

When doing multiple sets of an exercise, it is necessary to take a rest break (interval) between sets. This rest interval must be long enough to allow your muscles to recuperate sufficiently to do justice to the next set. The rest intervals should not be too long, however, because that will cause your body to begin to cool down and become susceptible to injuries. Additionally, excessively long rest intervals actually destroy the value of doing sets in the first place.

While competing bodybuilders sometimes rest as little as 10–15 seconds between sets, we feel that the minimum rest interval for most men and women training with weights should be 45 seconds. And while competitive weight lifters often rest three to five minutes between their maximum-effort sets, your longest rest interval should not exceed 90 seconds.

Generally speaking, we recommend a 60-second rest interval between sets, during which you should keep moving a little by walking slowly away from your weight or exercise apparatus and then walking back to it. Walking is better than sitting between sets, because movement actually improves blood circulation, and hence increases the rate of recuperation. This is true because muscle contractions in the extremities force blood past one-way valves in the vascular system, aiding the heart to circulate blood.

As you gain experience in weight training and bodybuilding, you will discover that you might need more rest between sets when you are doing leg and back exercises than when training your arms and shoulders. This is due to the fact that large muscle groups burn up more glycogen and oxygen when working than do smaller muscle groups. Therefore, it's logical that you will feel the need for longer rest intervals between sets of exercises for large muscle groups, for which you will use very heavy weights. Still, never allow yourself to rest more than 90 seconds between sets, or you will risk cooling off and injuring yourself.

EXERCISE FORM

As we mentioned earlier in this book, one of the beautiful things about weight training is that exercises exist to isolate resistance on single muscle groups, and even on segments of muscles. Weight training exercises can only accomplish this purpose, however, if each movement is done with strict form.

Strict form involves moving only the parts of the body intended to be used in each exercise, plus moving the weight over the full range of motion possible with each body joint involved in the movement. Only a full range of motion (from full extension to full contraction and back to full extension of each working muscle) and isolation of that motion will allow an exercise to fully stimulate the muscles being trained.

It is very easy to get into the habit of using a little kick of the knees or an unauthorized torso swing to help *cheat* up a weight heavier than you can use in strict exercise form. But at the beginning and intermediate levels of training, such cheating invariably removes stress from those muscles that should be receiving maximum stimulation.

In Chapter 5 we will teach you a method that advanced bodybuilders use to put *more* stress (not less) on a muscle by cheating. For now, however, move only those parts of your body actually involved in an exercise, and be very sure to do each weight training exercise over its full range of movement on every repetition.

CORRECT BREATHING

Beginning bodybuilders are inordinately concerned about the correct way to breathe while working out with weights. And in the past, weight training authorities have recommended a variety of breathing techniques for use while weight training. Some have suggested breathing in as the weight is lifted and out as it is lowered, while others recommend breathing out as the weight goes up and in as it comes down. With such polarity in suggestions for breathing technique, there is little wonder that beginners are confused about how to breathe.

We feel that you should focus your concentration on your working muscles during a set of

Demonstrating bench presses, Boyer raises his hips to cheat up a heavy weight, while Val uses strict form with a weight she can handle.

any exercise, not on your breathing. If you simply forget about worrying how to breathe, your breathing will take care of itself and supply your body with adequate oxygen. There are points along the range of motion of every exercise at which it's easiest to breathe in or out. Your subconscious mind will identify these points and coordinate your breathing with them quite efficiently and naturally, so you will not need to worry about when to breathe while performing a weight training movement.

It *is* essential to refrain from holding your breath while doing a heavy single effort of any exercise, and particularly the bench press. Keeping your glottis (throat air passage) closed while straining with a weight can cause something called the Valsalva Effect in which such great intrathoracic pressure is built up that veinous return of blood from the brain is prevented. This causes a blackout, which can be avoided by simply expelling air by grunting or groaning during the effort. Several deaths have been caused by lifters training alone and blacking out during a heavy bench press routine. The bar then crashed down across their necks, strangling them or fracturing neck vertebrae.

HOW MUCH WEIGHT?

A legitimate concern of all beginning male and female weight trainees is how much weight to use on each exercise in a training program. We will initially suggest starting weights for each exercise for both men and women in the beginning training program in Chapter 4. These exercise weights will be expressed in terms of percentages of an individual's body weight. Then once you have trained for 4–6 weeks, you will be able to accurately judge your starting poundages for new exercises in succeeding routines.

The percentages we suggest in Chapter 4 as starting weights for various exercises are based on the strength levels of average men and women. But due to either extensive recent athletic participation or several years of sedentary living, you may be stronger or weaker than average. Therefore, the weights you use for each exercise might need to be adjusted upward or downward after noting how well you perform with the suggested poundages in your first workout.

When you do a set of any exercise with the proper weight, it should be comfortably difficult to finish the lower guide number of repetitions required for the set. If you must actually struggle to complete this number of repetitions, or even are unable to do the full complement of reps, the weight you are using is too heavy and it should be reduced by 5–10 pounds. On the other hand, if you can easily do enough reps to reach the upper guide number, the weight is too light and should be appropriately increased.

To judge your starting weight for each exercise in the beginners' routine in Chapter 4, merely multiply your body weight by the listed percentage for your sex group. A man weighing 150 pounds will do a "30% movement" with 45 pounds. If you find your exercise weight coming out as anything but a multiple of five pounds once you calculate a specific percentage of your body weight, round your total *downward* to the nearest multiple of five pounds (e.g., 48½ pounds will be rounded downward to 45 pounds).

BREAK-IN AND MUSCLE SORENESS

If you attempt to jump directly into a full-scale weight training program without a sufficient preliminary break-in period, your muscles will become exceedingly sore. But by breaking in slowly and progressively to weight training in general—and to a new routine of exercises whenever you change training programs—you will be able to avoid such muscle soreness.

Actually, any type of exercise that exceeds the intensity level that your body is used to will induce muscle soreness. And this axiom applies to aerobic exercise, flexibility training, and even to such seemingly simple tasks as yard work equally as much as it applies to weight training. Regardless of the type of physical activity in which you engage, you should follow a gradual break-in process.

At the beginning of Chapter 4 you will find an exercise routine geared to complete beginners, both male and female. While multiple sets are listed for each exercise, you should begin a gradual break-in by doing only one set of every movement for the first week of your training. Be careful not to exceed the recommended starting poundages during the first week, even though they might feel quite light to you. Increasing your training weights before your second or third week of workouts is sure to cause muscle soreness, because it takes a week or two to fully condition them to using heavier weights.

Beginning with the second week of your weight training, you can start doing a second set of each exercise requiring two or three sets.

Then after another week or two you can add in the third set for all exercises requiring three sets. And finally, once you have completed a week of workouts using the full routine, we feel it's safe to begin increasing your training poundages.

Once you have broken in completely to a new training program and used it for several weeks, you will benefit from changing to a new one, as described in the next section of this chapter. Every time you begin a new training routine, you should also break into it gradually over a one-week period. Use lighter weights and a few less than the required number of sets the first workout day, and then gradually increase the sets and resistance until a week later you are up to full training intensity on your new routine.

Even if you follow proper break-in procedures, you might still experience some mild muscle soreness. If this soreness is severe enough to be a discomfort, you will find it easiest to relieve it by simply taking long, hot baths once or twice a day for two or three days.

SCHEDULE CHANGES

If you stay too long on the same training program, your mind and body can become stale, causing your progress on that routine to grind to a halt. To keep progressing at an optimum rate, therefore, it's best to change to a new training program each 4–6 weeks. Such schedule changes will keep your body and mind fresh and interested in each workout, insuring continued progress.

Some competitive bodybuilders, such as Franco Columbu, tend to use the same routines for months and even years, feeling that once they've found an effective training schedule they should stick to it. And at the opposite extreme, bodybuilders like Lou Ferrigno change their training schedules daily, following what can be called a "non-routine routine." These bodybuilders feel that they need such frequent changes in their training schedules to keep their interest levels high and their muscles unused to a set routine. Both of these aspects of the non-routine routine promote muscle growth.

Both of us feel that our interest levels are kept high enough to insure progress as long as we change our routines each month. Even though I may do a set routine for a month, I constantly vary certain aspects of it *from workout to workout.* For example, if I feel particularly strong one day, I'll use much heavier weights than on a low-energy day.

TRAINING DIARIES

Most athletes keep training diaries, and you will find this to be an excellent practice. An accurate and detailed training diary will give you an instantaneous concept of what progress you are making—particularly over the long haul—as well as vital clues to how effective various training and nutritional philosophies are on your body.

Often, it is difficult to see progress from week to week, let alone from one workout to the next. But with a good training diary you can quickly see how much strength you have gained in a particular exercise from one month (or year) to the next. And while you may become discouraged with a current lack of progress, you will find that you've actually made tremendous gains in strength over a period of a few months or years. If you keep records of your body weight and measurements—plus perhaps take photos of yourself each month and paste them in your diary—you can note long-term changes in your body exclusive of just strength increases.

A detailed training diary can also reveal what new training and/or dietary techniques result in especially quick gains in strength, muscle mass, and body fat loss. Used in this manner, a training diary can also help you to develop *training instinct,* or the ability to actually *feel* how new techniques are affecting your body. Instinctive training ability is essential to any competitive bodybuilder or advanced weight trainee.

At a minimum, your training diary can consist of the date of each workout and notes on what exercises, sets, reps, and training poundages you used in that workout. These can be noted in a spiral-bound notebook or inexpensive bound ledger or record book with a commonly used form of weight training shorthand. Using this shorthand, the first few lines of notes for a workout might look like this:

1. Sit-ups : 3 x50
2. Standing Calf Raise : 200, 3 x 15
3. Squat : 135 x 12, 165 x 10, 185 x 8, 205 x 6

In this form of weight training shorthand, the name of the exercise is almost always entered in full and the poundages, sets, and reps abbreviated. For your sit-ups in the above example, "3 × 50" means that you did three sets of 50 reps with no added resistance. When you use a constant weight for several sets, as in the standing calf raise, "200, 3 × 15" means that you used 200 pounds for three sets of 15 reps. Sometimes, this is also abbreviated "200 × 15 × 15 × 15," a system of notation that comes in handy when you fail to complete 15 reps on all three sets (e.g., "200 × 15 × 14 × 12," which is one set of 15 reps, one of 14 reps, and one of 12 reps, all with 200 pounds).

Weight training shorthand gets most tricky when you do sets of a particular exercise with differing weights and reps each set. In the above example for Squats, then, "135 × 12; 165 × 10; 185 × 8; 205 × 6" means that you did one set of 12 reps with 135 pounds, one set of 10 reps with 165, one set of 8 reps with 185, and one set of 6 reps with 205 pounds.

We have also found it valuable—particularly when peaking for contests—to keep a detailed daily nutritional record, including what food supplements we take. In such a dietary diary, you should note the times you eat, the foods you eat, the exact amount of each food or supplement consumed at each meal, and a daily total estimate for calories, grams of protein, grams of fat, and grams of carbohydrate eaten. If you keep a detailed nutrition diary year-round, you soon could develop an instinct for eating as well as for training.

At the beginning and intermediate training levels it can be valuable to include your body weight daily or weekly and your body's measurements each month. Measure the girth of each upper arm when flexed, each forearm, your chest or bustline (both "normal" and "expanded" with a full breath), your waist and hips, each thigh, and each calf.

Body measurements can change quickly during the first few months of regular training, but at the advanced level such measurements are virtually valueless. After a couple of years of training, these measurements change so slowly that recording them can be a negative emotional experience. At the advanced levels of weight training and bodybuilding, strength increases or

Boyer and Val record a workout in their training diary.

Numerous other types of notes can be kept in a fully detailed training and nutrition diary. Some of these are time and duration of each workout, your mood before and after training, an assessment of how each workout went, how long and well you slept, what outside stresses could be having a negative effect on your workouts, how much sun you took each day if you're a competitive bodybuilder peaking for a show, what compliments you have received on your improved appearance, what has particularly inspired you one day, and the type and duration of aerobic or other sports workouts you take.

One added incentive we discovered while keeping our own training diaries is to star (*) each exercise in which you increased your training poundage on particular workouts (e.g., "Bench Press: 120, 3 × 8*"). When you have a five-star workout, or one with more than five stars, you'll know conclusively that you're making *great* progress!

SAFETY

As we mentioned earlier, it is vital to thoroughly learn the procedures outlined in this section on weight training and bodybuilding safety. Several men have been killed in America while training alone and using heavy weights in an exercise called the bench press, and if proper safety procedures aren't followed it is possible to injure yourself fairly seriously while training with weights.

Considering the above circumstances, we would be very negligent in instructing you if we didn't emphasize the following five rules of weight training and bodybuilding safety:

1. *Always use a spotter when training with maximum weights.* This is particularly true when doing bench presses, an exercise in which you lie on your back on a bench and push a heavily loaded barbell from a position resting on your chest to straight arms' length directly above your chest. With a very heavy weight, it is possible to either black out or simply fail to push a weight completely up, and then the barbell can crash down across your chest, neck, or face.

An *alert* spotter stationed at the head end of your bench can prevent injuries when you black out or fail to complete a rep while bench press-

changes in appearance (which can take place with little or no change in measurements or body weight) are most important. For this reason, we recommend having photographs taken of yourself—even if they are just simple Polaroid shots—each month or two and pasting them in your diary. Over a period of several months or years, this photographic record will reveal an almost unbelievable change in the appearance of your body.

ing. Notice the emphasis placed on the word *alert*. A spotter or two can also rescue you when you fail to complete any of several variations of the squat exercise (all variations are fully described in Chapter 4).

2. *Always use collars on your barbells.* This is especially true when using an Olympic barbell. If your arms or legs extend or flex unevenly during a barbell exercise when you're not using collars, all of the plates can slide off the lower end of your barbell. This then causes the fully weighted end of the bar to whip viciously downward, resulting in wrenched knees, ankles, backs, shoulders, elbows, and wrists. Being sure to always use collars on your barbells (it's impossible to use dumbbells without collars in place) will prevent 100% of these injuries.

3. *Always warm up thoroughly before using maximum weights.* The importance of a thorough warm-up is discussed in detail with a warm-up program presented at the end of this chapter. For now, however, a warm-up makes your muscles, connective tissues (ligaments and tendons), and joints fully resistant to injuries that are inevitable when using heavy weights without a warm-up. A thorough warm-up also improves your neuromuscular coordination in all weight training movements, preventing loss of balance and the injuries caused by balance loss in some movements.

Val spots Boyer for a set of bench presses.

4. *Try to work out in a fully supervised weight training facility.* A qualified instructor can help you avoid improper biomechanical positions in your exercises, or otherwise sloppy exercise form and performance. Poor form can lead to many injuries. He or she can also act as your spotter when you use heavy weights in the bench press and other movements. Any institution which provides weight training facilities without also providing competent instruction and supervision can be found legally liable for injuries that a man or woman might incur while training there. If nothing else, a good weight training supervisor can keep weights picked up from the floor and placed in their proper racks, preventing trainees from tripping over them and injuring themselves.

5. *Be as fully informed as possible in how to correctly perform each exercise and how to train in general.* This rule is particularly important to follow if you can't work out under supervision. Be very careful in learning correct form in each exercise we give you in Chapter 3. Read the descriptions and compare them with the photos of us doing each exercise as many times as it takes you to completely understand every movement. If you are only slightly in doubt about how to perform an exercise, avoid doing it or make every effort to seek out an experienced bodybuilder or weight trainer who can observe your form in an exercise and advise you on how to correct any mistakes you might be making.

Similarly, you should be certain you fully understand every training technique explained in this chapter before you ever set foot inside a gym. Each training technique outlined in this chapter is fundamental to safe weight training. We feel we have clearly explained each basic training concept and technique in this chapter, but it is possible that you still might fail to understand one or two. In that case, we again urge you to seek out an experienced male or female bodybuilder or weight trainer who can clarify a misunderstood concept or technique for you.

SLEEP AND REST

Proper amounts of good quality sleep and rest are essential components of the body's recuperative cycle. And it's vital that your body is allowed to recuperate fully between workouts. Without full-body recuperation, you will fail to receive optimum results from your training.

While individual sleep requirements vary from as little as four hours to as much as 12 hours per night, you should shoot for seven to eight hours of sound sleep each day. This can consist of the amount of sleep you receive each night, plus a refreshing early afternoon nap or *siesta*. There is considerable wisdom in the old axiom that you should spend one third of your day in work, one third in leisure, and the other third in sound sleep. Still, don't be disturbed if you find six hours of sleep to be enough to fully refresh your mind and body, or eight hours of sleep too little to refresh you. Sleep requirements vary widely from individual to individual.

Regardless of the amount of sleep your body requires, proper amounts of sleep and rest are a requisite to full recuperation from a workout. Your body can most efficiently remove fatigue toxins and by-products from trained muscles and replenish glycogen (muscle fuel) and oxygen supplies only when you are sleeping or fully at rest. After all, it is only at rest that muscle hypertrophy occurs.

Therefore, we believe you should allow yourself two or three 15–20-minute rest breaks each day, during which you either sit motionless or lie down and fully relax your mind and body. These little pauses throughout the day will efficiently recharge your body's energy batteries, and you'll be able to go about your daily tasks with renewed vigor.

We also fully believe in maintaining a tranquil mind throughout the day. Nothing can fatigue you and disrupt your body's recuperative cycle

as quickly or as completely as mental stress. Keep from worrying and being uptight about your problems, and you will find yourself able to sleep better and rest more efficiently, which in turn will add up to accelerated progress from your weight training and bodybuilding workouts.

BASIC DIET TIPS

We could easily write—and perhaps soon may do so—a complete book on nutrition in relation to athletics, weight training, and bodybuilding, because it's a complicated topic and a factor that can improve sports performance or results from weight workouts by as much as 75%. Within the scope of this book, and because healthy nutrition is also requisite to your weight training and bodybuilding success, we will present 10 basic dietary tips in this chapter. Additionally, in Chapter 4 we will outline specific diets for gaining and losing weight, and in Chapter 5 we will outline the dietary methods of champion bodybuilders such as ourselves.

For now here are the 10 basic nutritional tips you can immediately begin utilizing to improve your diet at beginning and intermediate levels of weight training:

1. *Eat as wide a variety of foods as you possibly can.* Each food available to you has a unique combination of protein, fat and carbohydrate types, quality and contents, as well as unique combinations of vitamins, minerals, and trace elements. Therefore, by eating a wide variety of foods, you insure that your body is given a nutritionally well-balanced diet. Surprisingly, the average American eats a total of only 10–15 foods over and over. You could be far more healthy if you ate 25–30 foods on a regular, but rotational, basis.

2. *Eat all of your foods as fresh as possible.* At all costs, avoid canned and most packaged foods, which are generally loaded with sugar, salt, and preservatives. Even frozen foods have less nutritional value than the same foods served fresh. The thawing process that frozen foods undergo oxidizes (burns up) numerous nutrients that fresh foods have in abundance (such as vitamin C).

3. *Eat approximately one-half to one gram of protein per pound of body weight.* This protein should come primarily from animal sources,

Most bodybuilders believe that diet accounts for up to 75% of their success.

which contain protein of quality far superior to that from vegetable sources. If you do eat vegetable proteins—such as beans, peas, grains, and corn—at a meal, also consume animal protein (milk products, eggs, meat, poultry, or fish) with it. The animal-source protein will complement and improve the nutritional value of vegetable proteins.

4. *Limit your consumption of fats.* In particular, avoid animal fats that can clog up your arteries and may ultimately lead to cardiovascular disease. When metabolized for energy in your body, one gram of fat yields nine calories, more than twice as many as a gram of protein or carbohydrate (both yield four calories per gram). Thus, if you are trying to lose body weight by restricting your total caloric intake, you are far better off eating broiled fish or chicken (remove the fatty skin of all poultry before cooking it, however) than beef or pork, which are loaded with fat. Similarly, you should consume non-fat, rather than full-fat, milk products. And be sure to never fry foods, since the oil (at nine calories per gram) will be soaked up by the fish or poultry you are frying as if the food were a sponge.

5. *Your carbohydrate intake should come from* complex *carbohydrates (fresh vegetables,* fruit, and whole grains) rather than from refined *or* simple *carbohydrates (white sugar, white flour, and alcohol).* Simple carbohydrates are easily utilized by your body and provide little nutritional value other than calories. As a result, some nutritionists call sugar, flour, and alcohol sources of *empty calories.* Complex carbohydrates, on the other hand, require the burning of numerous calories just to process the foods and make the calories of fruits, vegetables, and whole grains available to your body. In some cases it actually requires more calories to digest a food than the food ultimately yields (e.g., celery and lettuce). And, complex carbohydrate foods are rich sources of vitamins and minerals in addition to calories. Fruits and vegetables also provide an abundance of natural food enzymes.

6. *Eat one or two servings of high-roughage foods (salad greens, pears, grain bran, etc.) each day.* Such roughage adds bulk to your stool, allowing regular and healthy bowel cleansing. The number of Americans who subsist almost totally on refined foods and suffer from constipation as a result is staggering.

7. *If your body has a tendency to retain excess water, reduce or eliminate your consumption of grains and/or milk products.* Ap-

As much as possible, prepare fresh foods—avoid all forms of refined carbohydrates.

proximately 95% of American men and women are mildly allergic to one or both of these food groups. And such mild food allergies have a tendency to retain water in the human body. If you have this allergy problem, only three to five days without eating grains and milk products can result in a water-weight loss of up to 5–10 pounds, regardless of how many calories you consume each day. And as long as you avoid allergenic foods in your diet, this weight will stay off. Val recently discovered that by eliminating milk and grains from her diet, she lost six pounds (all excess water) in only two weeks!

8. *Drink sufficient liquids—particularly distilled or purified water—each day.* You must drink at least 6–10 glasses of liquid per day, and even more if you are physically active and perspiring freely on a regular basis. By limiting your fluid intake, you can dehydrate your body and "lose" weight, but this is an unhealthy practice and weight losses from body dehydration are as temporary as your next few glasses of water. You may also be surprised to learn that when you are on a reduced-calorie diet you will actually lose body fat much more quickly when drinking plenty of water than you will when limiting your intake of fluids. Water plays a vital role in the metabolism of body fat.

9. *Use food supplements regularly, but conservatively.* Unless you have abused your body with long-term, poor nutritional practices, or are actually suffering from a specific dietary deficiency, you will never need to follow a program of megavitamin therapy. Numerous nutritional distributors have available multipacks consisting of several vitamin and mineral tablets/capsules enclosed in a small cellophane envelope. One such multipack contains more-than-adequate vitamins, minerals, and trace elements to meet the minimum daily requirements of any physically active man or woman. One to three multipacks a day will give you adequate and inexpensive insurance against nutritional deficiencies. Incidentally, for optimum absorption into the body, all vitamins and minerals should be taken with meals.

If you are competing on a high level as an athlete or bodybuilder, it's possible that you may need increased dosages of individual, water-soluble vitamins and minerals (particularly vitamin C, the B-complex vitamins, potassium, and calcium) when peaking. Since water-soluble vitamins and minerals stay in your body for only a short time before being eliminated through your urinary system, they should be taken frequently during the day. Never take extra amounts of the oil-soluble vitamins (A, D, E, and K), however; they can accumulate in your body and possibly reach toxic levels.

To insure the best quality of food supplementation, be sure that all of the supplemental minerals you consume have been chelated. Chelation is a biochemical process in which protein molecules are bonded to inorganic minerals, making them many times more usable by the human body than if the minerals had remained unchelated.

We also have noticed improved results from our workouts when we are using *timed-release* vitamins and mineral supplements, versus the normal type of supplements. Timed-release vitamins and minerals are formulated with various coatings that permit periodic release of the vitamins and minerals in your digestive tract, usually over 8–12-hour time periods, which is better for you nutritionally than having all of the supplements released in your stomach at once and then having none released for the next 8–12 hours.

If you have been wondering about using a protein supplement, we definitely recommend them, but not at beginning and intermediate levels of weight training. They are great for advanced bodybuilders, as well as for individuals who are having difficulty gaining weight.

10. *Take a long-range approach to lose weight.* If you desire to lose body fat, it is best to do this slowly and over a long period of time by incrementally and progressively reducing your total daily caloric intake until it is 15%–20% below its normal level. For every 3500 calories you fail to eat under the number your body needs to maintain its body weight, you will lose one pound of body fat. Reduced-calorie diets are far more effective, easier to follow, and healthier than so-called quick weight loss diets in which carbohydrate consumption is severely curtailed. (The process of dieting for body fat loss will be thoroughly explained in Chapter 4.)

TRAINING PARTNERS

As we pointed out in Chapter 1, it is ideal to have your spouse or girl-boyfriend as a training partner. Furthermore, it is much better to use a training partner than it is to work out alone. A partner can encourage you to greater efforts in your workouts, can be the spotter necessary for optimum safety when training with weights, can constantly monitor your exercise form, and will provide added incentive for regularity of training. (It's much more difficult to make up an excuse for missing a workout if your partner is ready to do it than it would be to miss a training session when you have only yourself to argue with about whether to go to the gym!)

In Chapter 5 we will discuss an advanced bodybuilding concept called *forced reps,* in which a partner helps you to squeeze out two or three more reps on an exercise than you would normally be able to do, simply by pulling up a little on the bar when it reaches the point where it would normally stop because of muscle failure. To most advanced bodybuilders, a partner who is used to his or her endurance levels when doing forced reps is as valuable as a Krugerrand each workout.

Unfortunately, a husband and wife, or boyfriend and girlfriend, often will have divergent goals in weight training or bodybuilding. In this case, it might be difficult to be training partners. When we are preparing for the World Couples' Bodybuilding Championship each year or for an important posing exhibition, we actually train together on the same routines, with Valerie simply using lighter training poundages than I use.

For most of the year, however, I am training for a succession of men's professional bodybuilding contests, while Val seeks merely to maintain good physical condition and an excel-

When Val isn't available, Boyer trains with Norm Crum.

lent appearance. Then, it is impractical for us to be full-fledged training partners. Still, we do our individualized workouts together as often as possible, because I feel a great deal of moral support from Val when we are in the gym together, even when I am training two or three times harder and much longer than she is.

WEIGHT TRAINING, AEROBICS, AND STRETCHING

Whether physical fitness, improved health and appearance, better athletic ability, or competitive bodybuilding is your ultimate goal, your weight training workouts are very compatible with aerobic training and sessions of stretching exercise. Combined in various proportions, these three primary types of physical exercise can result in an optimum level of physical conditioning.

While leading to lesser degrees of flexibility and aerobic endurance, weight training primarily develops muscular strength. There is, however, a special form of weight training we've already mentioned called *circuit training,* which allows you to simultaneously develop superior strength and great aerobic endurance. Still, even circuit training develops little body flexibility, and it offers less variety of exercise than can be

found in the normal range of aerobic activities.

Aerobic exercise is mild physical activity that can be comfortably carried on continuously for long periods of time, up to 30–60 minutes. To achieve a positive effect aerobically, this exercise must be sufficiently strenuous to elevate your pulse rate to at least 130 beats per minute; and aerobic exercise must be of sufficient duration to keep your pulse rate above 130 for at least 15 minutes. That will achieve for you what is called a *training effect.*

Ideally, your pulse rate should be kept in the range between 150 and 170 beats per minute for as long as possible. Exercise that induces a pulse rate of 150–170 beats per minute gives your cardiorespiratory system far greater benefit than physical movement that elicits a pulse rate of only 130. But if activity is so strenuous that it pushes your pulse much over 170 beats per minute, it ceases to be *aerobic*—literally, "with air," or within the body's ability to supply oxygen at the rate it is being consumed by the activity—and becomes *anaerobic,* which devel-

Riding a stationary bike is an important part of Boyer's aerobic workout program.

ops an *oxygen debt*. Such an oxygen debt quickly forces you to reduce the intensity of your exercise or to terminate it altogether.

Running is the most popular form of aerobic activity in our country, with an estimated 30 million Americans running on a regular basis. Runners do, however, experience numerous injuries. With each running step all or a large portion of your body weight is brought jarringly down on your feet, ankles, hips, lower spine, and all of your leg muscles. Because running results in so many injuries, sensible physical fitness devotees have turned to bicycling or swimming as their favorite aerobic activities. In each of these forms of aerobic exercise, all or most of the body weight is supported by the water or bicycle, which results in far less stress being placed on the legs and in fewer injuries.

Overall, we have found that variety is indeed the spice of life when it comes to doing aerobic exercise on a regular basis. We regularly rotate stationary bicycling, running, cycling, swimming, mountain hiking, aerobic dance classes, and nights out dancing to disco and rock-and-roll music in our aerobic exercise "programs." Such a great variety of types of exercise makes aerobics more interesting to both of us, which in turn induces us to do regular aerobic workouts.

A regular and progressive program of stretching movements is the best way to achieve maximum body flexibility. And in turn, better flexibility will both improve your athletic ability and reduce the number of injuries you might sustain from athletic participation. Bodybuilders have found that regular stretching of their muscles actually results in better physique development.

A good stretching program should take you only 15–20 minutes to complete, and stretching serves as an excellent warm-up for either weight training or aerobic exercise. Additionally, you will benefit most from stretching workouts if you do them on a daily basis. That's why we include stretching in our weight training and aerobic workouts six days per week.

WEIGHT TRAINING WARM-UPS

As we previously mentioned, it is essential to undertake a thorough warm-up before any heavy, weight training session. Such a warm-up will thoroughly prepare your body's joints and

skeletal muscles for the heavy stress of a weight workout. A proper warm-up will prevent weight training injuries, allow your muscles to operate more efficiently and to lift heavier weights, and dramatically improve your neuromuscular coordination over what it is when your body is cold.

In our experience, the best warm-up for a heavy weight training session lasts 10–15 minutes and combines aerobic activity, stretching exercises, and calisthenics movements. Then a little light weight training should be done before tackling heavy, workout poundages. Here is the warm-up that we have developed for use prior to our own bodybuilding workouts:

1. Rope Skipping (or Jogging in Place): 3–5 minutes
2. Hamstring and Lower Back Stretching: 30–40 seconds to each side
3. Towel Dislocates: 3–5 reps slowly in each direction
4. Jumping Jacks: 30–50 repetitions
5. Floor Dips (Knee Dips for women): 30–50 repetitions
6. Upper Back Stretching: 30–40 seconds
7. Freehand Squats: 20–30 repetitions
8. Thigh Stretching: 30–40 seconds to each side
9. Calf Stretching: 30–40 seconds to each side
10. Trunk Twisting: 30–50 repetitions in each direction

We perform this warm-up routine in a continuous manner, resting only 5–10 seconds between exercises to assume the body position for the next movement. Done in such a continuous manner, this program should take you only about 10 minutes to complete. At the end of it, you will have broken a sweat and reached a point where you are reasonably warmed up.

After this warm-up we either do our stretching program or our weight training abdominal workout as a further warm-up. Often we do our stretching before aerobic workouts, in which case we proceed on weight days directly to doing our abdominal routine. When we do our stretching before a bodybuilding or weight training workout, we immediately follow the stretching exercises with our abdominal routine.

Once we have completed our abdominal training, we move directly into our weight workout, being sure we rest no more than 60 seconds between sets. If we rested more than 60 seconds, we would risk having our bodies cool down in mid-workout, totally negating the value of our warm-ups.

When we are using particularly heavy weights in an exercise, as I invariably do (I use up to 1200 pounds on one of my thigh building exercises), we do one to three warm-up sets with lighter weights in each heavy movement before tackling maximum training poundages. When we do one warm-up set, it is usually 8–10 reps with 50%–75% of our maximum exercise weight for the movement, while a two-set warm-up consists of one set of 10–12 reps at 50% and one set of 8–10 reps at 75% of maximum in an exercise. In a full, three-set warm-up for any exercise, we recommend one set of 12–15 reps at 50%, one set of 10–12 reps at 75%, and one set of 8–10 reps at 90% of maximum.

Actually warming up with weights in some exercises usually becomes necessary only when you have developed a great degree of strength.* Warm-ups with weights should be done for at least the first basic exercise that you do for each muscle group every workout.

We realize that some readers will be unfamiliar with a few of the exercises in our warm-up program, so to conclude this section, here are illustrations and detailed descriptions of those ten exercises.

ROPE SKIPPING/JOGGING IN PLACE

These two exercises are identical in their effect on the body as warm-ups, so you can either choose your favorite, or alternate them each workout. Everyone has skipped rope, so it needs little description. Simply start out slowly and then gradually build up the height of your jumps and the pace of your movement over a three- to five-minute period. You can jump on both feet simultaneously, alternate feet, or run as you skip rope. And if you are a real pro at skipping rope, you can *double turn* and/or cross your hands in front of your torso as you are skipping.

Jogging in place should begin with slow, easy steps that are only a little faster than a walking

pace and in which your feet are lifted only 2–3 inches off the floor each step. Then over a three- to five-minute period, you should gradually increase the speed of your jogging in place and the height you raise your knees on each step. As an alternative to jogging in place, you can, of

---

*We would define this for a man as being able to bench press 100% of his body weight and squat 130% of body weight for 8–10 repetitions; a woman's percentages for the same movements and repetitions are 75% and 100% respectively.

Hamstring and lower back stretching.

course, actually take a five- or ten-minute jog around your neighborhood before continuing with the rest of your warm-up.

Both skipping rope and jogging in place stimulate blood circulation and begin warming up the thigh and calf muscles.

HAMSTRING AND LOWER BACK STRETCHING

This stretching movement, as its name implies, stretches the hamstring muscles on the backs of your thighs and the muscles of your lower back. Begin by spreading your feet about three to four feet apart. Keeping your legs straight, lean slowly toward your left thigh, grasping your leg with your hands and gently pulling your torso toward your thigh. On all stretching exercises, stretch until you begin to feel a slight pain in the muscles being stretched. Then back off slightly in your stretch and hold that sub-pain, stretched position for 30–40 seconds. Repeat this stretch toward your other leg.

TOWEL DISLOCATES

This exercise loosens up the muscles of your shoulders, back, chest, and arms. You will need only a towel or three-foot length of rope as your equipment. Begin by standing erect and grasping the ends of the towel (or hold the rope with your hands an equivalent distance apart). Then extend your arms overhead so the towel or rope is taut. Throughout this movement your arms must remain straight and you must keep the towel taut.

From this basic starting position, move your hands slowly in semicircles backward and downward, "dislocating" your shoulders in the process, until the towel contacts your lower back or buttocks. Then slowly return along the same path until you are back to the starting point. Repeat this movement for the required number of repetitions.

JUMPING JACKS

This fairly complicated exercise is an excellent warm-up movement for virtually every muscle of your body. Begin by standing erect with your feet together and with arms at your sides. Keeping your arms straight throughout the movement, simultaneously hop up a few inches, spread your legs a comfortable distance apart

Towel dislocates: Boyer, start; Val, finish.

(two to three feet apart is about average), and swing your arms directly out to the sides and upward in semicircles until your hands touch lightly directly above your head. Just as your hands touch each other, your feet should hit the floor in the position with your legs spread. Bend your knees slightly to absorb the mild impact of landing on the floor, then immediately spring upward again and return your arms and legs simultaneously to the starting point. Again bend your legs to absorb the impact of your landing and immediately launch yourself into a second repetition of the movement. With a minimum of practice you will be able to do 30–50 repetitions of this excellent warm-up exercise.

FLOOR DIPS

This commonly used exercise places stress on the chest, shoulder, and triceps muscles. Men should start the movement supporting their straight bodies on their toes and straight arms as illustrated. To lessen the severity of the exercise, women should start by supporting their straight torsos and thighs on their knees (bend your legs to remove your lower legs from the movement) and on straight arms. Both men and women should have their hands set at shoulder width and with their fingers pointed directly forward. The feet or knees should be set at shoulder width or slightly more narrow.

From these starting positions, bend your arms and lower your torso downward until your chest lightly touches the floor, and then immediately push yourself back up to the starting point. Be sure your upper arms travel directly out to the sides as you bend your arms in the exercise, and be careful to keep your torso and legs held in a straight line at all times. Repeat this movement for the required number of repetitions.

UPPER BACK STRETCHING

This movement is best done with a partner. Correctly performed, it stretches all of the muscles of the upper back, plus the biceps and forearms. Start by sitting on the floor facing your partner and with your feet spread at about shoulder width and placed sole-to-sole against your partner's feet. Then either firmly clasp each other's hands or both grasp a broomstick (in this case, one partner's hands must be placed on the broomstick inside the hands of the other partner). At the start of the exercise both partners' hands will be above their feet.

From this basic starting position, one partner will lean backward, pulling the other forward into a fully stretched position in which the arms are completely straight, the head is lowered between the arms, and a stretching sensation is felt in the upper back muscles. To allow the stretching partner to reach a fully stretched position, the partner leaning back may need to also bend his or her arms to some degree. Hold the fully stretched position for 30–40 seconds and then reverse positions.

If you can't find a partner with whom you can perform this stretch, you can do a satisfactory version of it by yourself with a door handle. (Please be careful; make sure the handle is not loose!) Simply face the edge of the door and grasp a knob of the handle in each hand. Step back two or three feet and straighten your arms, lowering your head between your arms. Then simply maintain this position and lower your

Jumping jacks: Boyer, start; Val, finish.

Floor dips: Boyer, start (men's style); Val, finish (women's style).

hips by slowly bending your legs until you feel a good stretch in your upper back muscles.

FREEHAND SQUATS

This is an easy exercise that you can use to stress the muscles of your thighs, hips, and buttocks. It's often done as a weight training exercise while holding a barbell across the shoulders. Start by standing erect with your feet set at shoulder width and your toes pointed outward at 45-degree angles on each side. Extend your arms forward at shoulder level and hold them in this position throughout the move-

Upper back stretching.

ment to help balance your body.

From this starting position, simply bend your knees and sink into a fully squatting position, trying to keep your torso upright and your feet flat on the floor as you squat down. Return to the starting point by straightening your legs and repeat the movement 20–30 repetitions. If you can't do this squat with your feet flat on the floor, then perform it balanced on your toes. Regardless of the position of your feet, however, be sure that your knees travel outward at 45-degree angles on each side directly over your feet as you bend and straighten your legs.

THIGH STRETCHING

It always feels good to stretch the thigh muscles after doing squats, whether you have done them freehand or with a 500-pound barbell held behind your neck. Stand next to a table, an upright pole, or metal rod. Grasp this object with your left hand to balance your body during the stretch. Then fully bend your right leg and reach back with your right hand to grasp the toes of your right foot.

To stretch your thigh muscles, merely pull directly upward with your right hand on your right foot until you feel a strongly stretched sensation in your right thigh muscles. Hold this

stretch for 30–40 seconds and then repeat it for your left leg.

CALF STRETCHING

The calf muscles at the back of your lower legs can be stretched out either with both legs at once or one leg at a time. Start by standing about two to three feet back from a wall, facing the wall. Keeping your legs and torso in one long straight line, lean forward and place your hands on the wall a little below shoulder level. With your arms straight, you may feel a slight stretch in your calves at this point while your feet are flat on the floor, but chances are good that you'll need to inch your feet even farther from the wall to achieve a good stretch in your calves.

You can stretch one calf at a time with greater overall stretching intensity in this same position simply by bending one knee. You'll immediately feel a stronger stretching sensation in the calf of the leg held straight. Maintain this stretch for 30–40 seconds and repeat it for the other leg.

TRUNK TWISTING

This movement loosens up the lower back and abdomen, as well as the muscles of the torso

Freehand squats: Val, start; Boyer, finish.

Thigh stretching: Boyer, start; Val, finish.

and arms. Start by standing erect with your feet set at shoulder width and your toes pointed directly forward. Extend your arms straight out to the sides at shoulder level and keep them straight throughout the movement. Then quickly twist at your waist from side to side as far to the right and left as possible for 30–50 repetitions in each direction. As you are twisting, keep your hips as motionless as possible.

Trunk twisting is also done as a weight training movement, usually while seated on a bench and holding a light barbell or broomstick behind the neck and across the shoulders.

SOURCES OF ADDITIONAL INFORMATION

As extensive and authoritative as the information contained in this book might be, it can still take you only a certain distance into weight training and bodybuilding before leaving you to continue on your own. Then you must utilize one or more sources of additional information on weight training, bodybuilding, and nutrition.

The first of these sources is the growing number of books on weight training and bodybuilding, many of which have been authored by

Calf stretching: Val, one leg; Boyer, two legs.

Trunk twisting: Boyer, start; Val, finish.

champion bodybuilders. A second source of additional information is the large number of weight training and bodybuilding magazines that can be found on newsstands or in bookstores and shopping markets.

Of all these magazines, the two best are *Muscle & Fitness* and *Shape,* both published by Joe Weider. *Muscle & Fitness* focuses on weight training and bodybuilding for men and women, while *Shape* focuses on the health-and-fitness lifestyle strictly for women. We regularly write articles for both of these magazines, and only for these magazines.

As we've previously hinted, experienced male and female weight trainees are excellent sources of information. This is particularly true when the men and women you consult are champion bodybuilders such as ourselves. Most large gyms have such competitors as members, or you can attend one or several of the hundreds of training seminars and nutrition lectures that we (and other top male and female bodybuilders) present virtually every week across America.

WHAT'S NEXT?

We realize that this has been a very long and information-filled chapter, but it was so by necessity. Very simply, there is a large amount of basic information that every beginning weight trainee or bodybuilder must master before setting foot in a gym. Therefore, we strongly suggest that you review this chapter a second time before venturing into a gym. This way you can be confident that you are armed with sufficient basic information to safely receive maximum results from your weight training workouts.

In Chapter 3 we will introduce you to a basic pool of over 50 weight training exercises along with their variations, which will give you more than 100 different training movements that you can use in your weight workouts. Then, looking even farther ahead in this book, we will combine many of the exercises from Chapter 3 into a variety of beginning, intermediate, and advanced weight training programs in Chapter 4.

3
Your Weight Training Exercises

Counting variations on basic movements, there are approximately 100 weight training and bodybuilding exercises described in this chapter. Ultimately, each exercise should be fully mastered, because they all will be used at some point by you in the months and years ahead as you continue with your weight training and bodybuilding workouts.

We have included the most commonly used exercises in this chapter, but they only represent the tip of the iceberg in terms of the total number of resistance exercises available for your use. In his popular book, *Keys to the Inner Universe,* Bill Pearl lists hundreds of weight training exercises for each muscle group. Since there are so many movements in existence, we suggest that you use the ones we outline here only as a basic exercise pool, and then gradually add to that pool over the years.

Every exercise in this chapter is illustrated with photographs in which we demonstrate the correct starting and finishing positions of the movement. These photographs are accompanied by detailed written descriptions of how to do each exercise. Each exercise is keyed explicitly to the muscle group or groups it stresses. In addition, our text will supply suggestions that will help you make most exercises even more effective for your body than mere pictures can provide.

By comparing the photographs with the written descriptions for each exercise, then practicing the movements without weights, you should have little difficulty in learning how to perform each weight training movement correctly. If it worries you that you might be incorrectly performing an exercise, simply have an experienced male or female weight trainee or bodybuilder check out your exercise form for one or two workouts. And if you train in a large gym, and a highly experienced man or woman suggests a form correction—as we often do when we see novices making mistakes—make the suggested change immediately. Using improper biomechanical position in some exercises can be injurious to your body.

ABDOMINAL EXERCISES

Sit-Ups

Sit-ups stress the front abdominal muscles,

particularly the upper half of the *abdominis rectus*.

The primary mistake most beginning and intermediate trainees make is throwing their head and shoulders forward to assist the upward movement. This simply removes stress from the abdominal muscles, so be sure to slowly curl up each time. You can also do sit-ups with a twisting motion to each side on alternate reps. To increase resistance on your abdominal muscles when doing sit-ups, you can either hold a weight behind your neck, or raise the foot end of your abdominal bench.

Leg Raises

This movement stresses the front abdominal muscles, particularly the upper half of the *abdominis rectus*.

To add resistance to this movement, simply raise the head end of the bench in gradual increments. The higher the angle of the bench, the greater the stress you will put on your front abdominal muscles with leg raises. As a variation on the basic leg raise movement, you can raise your legs alternately (raise one up fully, then as it starts to come down, begin raising the other one; this results in a scissors movement).

Knee-Ups

Knee-ups place emphasis on the front abdominal muscles. Val has found this to be a particularly effective exercise for eliminating lower tummy bulge.

This movement is of less intensity than standard leg raises. To make this movement more intense, you can hold a light dumbbell between your feet by simply pressing your feet together.

Hanging Frog Kicks

This movement emphasizes the entire front abdominal muscle group, particularly the lower section.

There is a tendency for the body to begin swinging during this movement. In such a case, a training partner can prevent this swinging simply by grasping your hips. To stress your external oblique and intercostal muscles, this exercise can also be done by twisting, which

involves raising your legs alternately to each side as you pull up your knees during the movement. Lately this variation has become one of my favorite abdominal exercises.

Side Bends

This exercise tones the external oblique muscles at the sides of your waist.

This movement should ordinarily be done with light resistance and for very high repetitions (50–100 to each side), since heavy resistance and lower repetitions can make the external oblique muscles grow very quickly, resulting in a wide-waisted look. To add resistance to side bends, either hold a dumbbell in each hand, or hold a dumbbell in one hand and place your free hand behind your neck (alternate hands in which the dumbbell is held each set).

Seated Twisting

This exercise tones the external oblique muscles at the sides of your waist. It also loosens up the lower spine.

This movement is often done standing, which—as we have mentioned—makes it difficult to keep the hips from moving, thereby making the movement ineffective. The only way to restrain your hips while standing is to do the movement in a bent-over position.

CALF EXERCISES

Barbell Calf Raise

This simple movement exercises the whole of the *gastrocnemius* muscle of your lower legs.

Note: You will need a 2″ × 4″ or 4″ × 4″ block of wood—or its equivalent—for all calf movements, because it allows a trainee to stretch his or her heels below the toes, resulting in a longer range of movement in all calf exercises.

On this and all other calf exercises, you should vary your foot position from set to set to add variety to the types of stress you place on your calves. The basic foot positions are with your feet parallel to each other, with your toes pointed outward at 45-degree angles and with your toes pointed inward at 45-degree angles. You can also vary the distance between your

Start—Lie on your back on the floor or on an abdominal bench and hook your toes under a heavy piece of furniture or the strap or roller of the bench. Bend your legs at a 30-degree angle, which will remove the stress that straight-legged sit-ups can place on your lower back. Interlace your fingers behind your neck and hold your hands in this position throughout the movement.

Sit-Ups

Finish—Slowly curl your torso off the floor or board, lifting first your head, then your shoulders, your upper back, and your lower back. As soon as your torso has assumed a position at a 90-degree angle to the bench or floor, slowly lower yourself back to the starting position by simply reversing the movement that you used to raise your torso. Repeat the movement for the required number of repetitions.

Leg Raises

Start—Lie on your back on the floor or on an abdominal bench. Grasp the roller or strap on the abdominal bench with your hands, or grasp a heavy piece of furniture behind your head. Slightly unlock your legs to take potential strain off your lower back.

Finish—Raise your legs so your feet travel in a semicircle from the floor or board to a position with your thighs at a 90-degree angle to your torso. Lower slowly back to the starting position, touching your heels lightly to the bench or floor. Then immediately initiate another repetition. Repeat the movement for the required number of repetitions.

Knee-Ups

Start—Sit at the end of a flat exercise bench, or on the edge of any chair. Your buttocks should be placed right at the edge of the bench or chair. Extend your legs forward and downward at an angle between 30 and 45 degrees below an imaginary line drawn parallel to the floor. Lean your torso backward until it is along an imaginary line drawn through your legs (i.e., your body is straight). Brace your torso into this position with your hands by grasping the sides of the bench or chair. Press your legs together and keep them together throughout the movement.

Finish—Keeping your torso in the same position, bend your knees and pull your thighs and knees up to your chest. Pause for a second in the top position and return back to the starting point. Repeat the movement for the required number of repetitions.

Hanging Frog Kicks

Start—Stand below a chinning bar. Jump up and grasp the chinning bar with a shoulder-width grip. Your palms should be facing forward. At the start of this movement, your body should be entirely straight.

Finish—Keeping your arms straight throughout the movement, slowly raise your knees up to your chest, bending your legs in the process. Hold the top position for a moment and then return back to the starting point. Repeat for the required number of repetitions.

Hanging Frog Kicks also can be done by alternately twisting legs to each side.

Side Bends

Start—Stand erect and spread your feet slightly wider than shoulder width. Place a broomstick or unloaded barbell behind your neck and wrap your arms around it. Keep your legs straight throughout the movement, and try not to move your hips from side to side as you do your side bends.

Finish—Bend as far directly to the right side as you can. Return to the starting point and then bend as far to the left side as you can. Rhythmically bend back and forth for the required number of repetitions.

Seated Twisting

Start—Sit on a flat exercise bench and wrap your legs around the upright legs of the bench. This will prevent your hips from moving, something that doesn't occur when this movement is done standing. Place a broomstick or unweighted barbell behind your neck and wrap your arms around it.

Finish—Twist at the waist as far to the left as possible. Then immediately twist as far as you can to the right. Alternate rhythmically from right to left for the required number of repetitions to each side.

feet during the movement. There is a considerable difference in the type of stress placed on your calves when your feet are close together from what is placed on your calves when your feet are placed farther apart.

Standing Calf Machine

This movement stresses the same muscles as the barbell calf raise, but without the balance problems inherent in doing the movement with a barbell.

Use the toe positions and foot spacings mentioned for barbell calf raises. This movement can also be done with one foot at a time.

Seated Calf Machine

This is the most effective movement for stressing the *soleus* muscles lying under the *gastrocnemius* muscles of the calves. The *soleus* muscles can be fully contracted only when the knees are bent at 90-degree angles.

The *soleus* often seems to respond better to lower reps (8–10) than does the *gastrocnemius*. If you don't have access to a seated calf machine, you can still do this exercise with a block, barbell, towel, and flat exercise bench. Simply roll the towel around the middle of the bar to pad it, place your toes on the block, place the padded barbell across your knees, and sit down on the edge of the bench. Then do your calf raises from this position.

Donkey Calf Raise

This exercise develops all of the calf muscles.

Biomechanically, your training partner will feel heavier if he or she sits back toward the edge of your hips, rather than forward toward your shoulders. If your partner isn't heavy enough, he or she can hold a dumbbell or heavy barbell plate against your lower back during the movement to supply additional resistance.

Toe Press

This movement also exercises all of the muscles at the backs of your lower legs.

This movement can also be done on three other types of leg press machines: Universal Gym, Nautilus, and the 45-degree angled machine. It is equally effective on all four types of leg press machines.

One-Leg Toe Raise

This movement is simple in that it can be done with just a single dumbbell and either a block of wood or a stair riser. It exercises all of the calf muscles.

Many top bodybuilders agree that this is one of the best of all calf exercises. One reason for this is the fact that your concentration needn't be split between two exercising legs. It can be focused in on working one calf muscle at a time. Because of this improved concentration factor, I do many exercises with only one leg or arm at a time.

THIGH EXERCISES

Squat

This is the best of all lower body exercises, and perhaps one of the best of all weight training and bodybuilding movements. It strongly stresses the muscles of the front thighs, the hips, the buttocks, and the lower back. It places secondary stress on the hamstring, calf, and upper back muscles. The abdominal muscles are also called into play to stabilize the body in position during the movement.

Keeping your eyes focused on a point at head height will prevent your face from turning downward, which in turn prevents your back from rounding. If you allow your back to round during a squat, you will find your lower back can be easily injured. Wearing a weight lifting belt while squatting will help prevent rounding your back. Some trainees with inflexible ankles find it difficult to do squats flat-footed. In such a case, it is best to rest your heels on a 2" × 4" board for better balance during a squat.

Partial Squats

The emphasis in partial squats is the same as for regular squats, except that much heavier weights will be handled over a shorter range of motion than with regular squats. This builds greater ligament and tendon strength.

Barbell Calf Raise

Start—Stand erect with a barbell balanced across your shoulders and behind your neck as illustrated. Place your toes and the balls of your feet on the wood block. Stretch your heels as far below your toes as possible. Keep your knees locked throughout the movement. Your toes should be pointed directly ahead and your heels should be 6 to 8 inches apart.

Finish—Simply rise up as high on your toes as possible. Lower back down to the starting position and repeat the movement for the required number of repetitions.

Standing Calf Machine

Start—Place your toes and the balls of your feet on the toe board and bend your legs enough to fit your shoulders under the yokes of the machine. Place your hands either on the handles provided, or rest them along the movement arms of the machine. Straighten your legs and sag your heels as far below your toes as possible.

Finish—Rise as high on your toes as possible. Return to the starting position and repeat for the required number of repetitions.

Calf raise with toes straight ahead.

Calf raise with toes out.

Calf raise with toes in.

**Calf
Machine
Variations**

Seated Calf Machine

Start—Sit in the calf machine and adjust the knee pad upward or downward to accommodate the length of your shins. Place your toes and the balls of your feet on the toe board and force your knees under the knee pads. Rise slightly up on your toes and then release the stop bar by pushing it forward. Sag your heels as far below your toes as possible.

Finish—Rise up and down on your toes to the fullest extent possible in each direction.

Donkey Calf Raise

Start—Place your toes and the balls of your feet on a block and then bend forward until your torso is parallel to the floor. Brace your hands on a flat exercise bench to keep your torso in this position. Then have a heavy training partner jump up astride your hips. Keep your legs straight throughout the movement.

Finish—Rise up as high as possible on your toes. Lower yourself back down to the starting position and repeat the movement for the required number of repetitions.

Toe Press

Start—Lie on your back beneath a vertical leg press machine, positioning your hips directly under the moveable part of the apparatus. Bend your legs and place the toes and balls of your feet on the board. Straighten your legs and keep them straight throughout the movement.

Finish—Extend your feet to the maximum. Return them to a fully flexed position and repeat the movement for the required number of repetitions.

One-Leg Toe Raise

Start—Stand with the ball and toes of your left foot on a block of wood or a stair riser, and keep your left leg straight throughout the movement. Bend your right leg to get it up and out of the movement. Hold a dumbbell in your left hand and balance your body during the movement by grasping the railing or a solid object with your right hand. Sag the heel of your left foot down as far below your toes as you can.

Finish—Rise up as high as you can on the toes of your left foot. Lower back to the starting position and repeat for the required number of repetitions. Be sure to do an equal number of sets and reps for your right leg.

With all forms of partial squats—as well as with regular squats eventually—the weight that you use will be so heavy that you won't be able to get it up behind your neck unassisted. In such a case squat racks are used. These racks are constructed in such a manner that a light barbell can be placed on them and loaded up to a heavy weight. Then you need merely step under the bar, position it across your shoulders, straighten your legs to bear the weights, step back a few feet, and do your squats. Then when you have finished your set, you can merely replace the barbell on the rack.

Lunges

Lunges strongly stress the upper thigh muscles, as well as the hips and buttocks. Champion bodybuilders do a lot of lunges to bring out upper thigh cuts. Val has discovered them to be a key movement for firming and toning a woman's hips, buttocks, and upper thighs.

Lunges can also be done freehand, or while holding two dumbbells down at the sides of your waist. Some bodybuilders also do them by stepping up on a flat exercise bench with their front foot at the start of the movement.

Hack Squat

This movement stresses all of the front thigh muscles, particularly those just above the knees. Bodybuilders consider the hack squat to be a key movement for achieving muscularity in the front thigh.

On all squatting-type exercises—and particularly on hack squats—you can do the movements in *non-lock* fashion. This involves coming up only to within about six inches of a straight-legged position. Doing squats in non-lock fashion keeps *continuous tension* on your front thigh muscles. Continuous tension, which is explained in detail in Chapter 5, is a very valuable training technique for bringing out the maximum in front thigh cuts.

Leg Extension

This is an isolation movement that places stress almost exclusively on the quadriceps muscles on the fronts of your thighs.

Holding your legs straight at the top of this movement takes advantage of a technique called *peak contraction*. This technique also is fully discussed in Chapter 5. Peak contraction is a valuable, advanced training technique that will accelerate your muscle mass gains. You also can do this movement one leg at a time, which is a favorite technique of mine.

Leg Curl

This is an isolation movement that places stress almost exclusively on the *biceps femoris* muscles (hamstrings) at the back of your thighs. It places secondary emphasis on calf muscles.

A common mistake when doing leg curls is to allow the hips to come off the bench when a repetition becomes difficult to complete. This robs the movement of much of its effectiveness. As with leg extension, peak contraction is important, and the movement can be done one leg at a time. Some gyms have a leg curl machine in which leg curls are actually done one leg at a time while standing up. This particular variation of leg curls gives superior stimulation to the *biceps femoris* muscles.

BACK EXERCISES

Shrugs

Shrugs primarily stress the powerful trapezius muscles (traps) of the upper back, with secondary emphasis placed on the upper pectoral muscles.

You can get more freedom of movement when doing shrugs if you hold two dumbbells in your hands instead of a barbell. Then you can actually do what is called rotating shrugs, in which you rotate your shoulders either upward and backward, then downward and forward, or in the opposite direction. There is a special Nautilus machine designed strictly for doing shrugs. And many bodybuilders prefer to do shrugs at the bench press station of a Universal Gym. In this variation, you will find a completely different *feel* in your traps when doing shrugs facing

Text continues on page 67.

Squat

Start—Stand erect with your feet set at shoulder width and your toes pointed outward at 45-degree angles. Place a barbell across your shoulders behind your neck and balance it in position with your hands. Tense all of your back muscles and focus your eyes on a point on the wall at head height.

Finish—Keep your torso upright throughout the movement and slowly bend your legs to squat down into a position where your thigh bones are below an imaginary line drawn parallel to the floor. As you are squatting down, be sure that your knees travel out at 45-degree angles directly over your feet. Without bouncing in the bottom position, slowly return to the starting point and repeat the movement for the required number of repetitions.

Partial Squats

Start—The starting position for partial squats is identical to that of regular squats in all respects.

Finish—Partial squats are done sinking down either three-quarters of the way to a position where the thigh bones would be parallel to the floor, half the way down, or a quarter of the way down. The less the distance you travel downward on a squat, the greater the amount of weight you can use in the movement. There is also a special partial squat called a bench squat, which is done straddling a flat exercise bench and squatting down until the buttocks lightly touch the bench, then returning to the starting position.

Start—The starting position for lunges is the same as for squats, except that the toes should be pointed directly forward.

Finish—Step forward two to three feet with your left leg, keeping your right leg as straight as possible, and then bend your left leg fully. This will stretch the muscles on the front of your right thigh, stimulate the muscles on the front of your left thigh, and stress the hip and buttock muscles of your left leg. At the bottom position of this movement, your left knee should be three to six inches ahead of your left ankle. From this position, push back to the starting point and do the next rep by stepping forward with your right leg. Alternate legs until you have done the required number of repetitions for both legs.

Lunges

Hack Squat

Start—Place your feet in the middle of the hack machine footboard with your heels about six to eight inches apart and your toes pointed outward at 45-degree angles on each side. Bend your knees fully and place your back flat against the moveable platform. Grasp the handles at the lower outside edges of the platform and hold them with your arms straight throughout the movement. Your feet should be flat on the platform and they should remain that way throughout the exercise.

Finish—Slowly straighten your legs, which will cause the platform to slide upward along with your torso. (It slides on little rollers, so you'll find that it provides minimum friction against the movement.) Return to the starting point and repeat for the required number of repetitions.

Leg Extension

Start—Sit in a leg extension machine (it can be freestanding, part of a Nautilus machine, or part of a Universal Gym machine) with your knees hanging over the edge of the machine toward the movement arm. Then hook your insteps under the lower set of rollers (on the Nautilus machine there will be only one set of rollers). Grasp the handles at the sides of the seat you are sitting in or the sides of the table on which you are sitting. Sit erect.

Finish—Slowly straighten your legs fully. Hold this straight position for a count or two and then lower slowly back to the starting point. Repeat the movement for the required number of repetitions.

Leg Curl

Start—Lie facedown on a leg curl machine (it can be freestanding, a Nautilus machine, or part of a Universal Gym machine) with your knees at the edge of the padded bench closest to the movement arm of the machine. Hook your heels under the upper set of rollers (there will be only one set of rollers on the Nautilus machine). Grasp the handles at the sides of the bench at the head end, or the sides of the padded bench itself. Fully straighten your legs.

Finish—Slowly bend your legs as fully as possible. Hold the top position for a count or two and then lower back to the starting position.

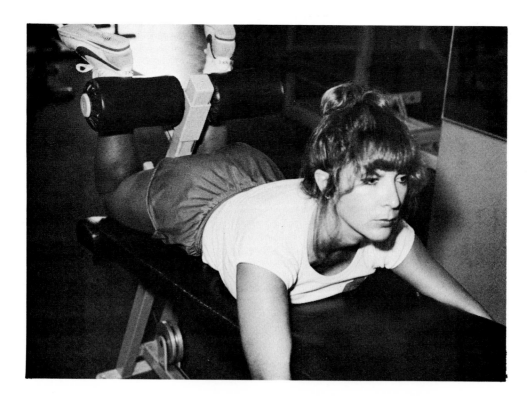

Text continued from page 60.

away from the machine than you will when facing the machine.

Upright Rowing

This movement strongly stresses the trapezius and deltoid muscles, with secondary emphasis placed on the biceps and all of the forearm muscles.

Two variations of upright rowing exist. In the first, the movement is done with a floor pulley (either on a Universal Gym machine, or on a freestanding floor pulley) and a short, straight bar handle, which is grasped as if it were a barbell during the movement. The second variation is done while holding two dumbbells instead of a barbell.

Deadlifts

The regular version of deadlifts strongly influences the erector spinae muscles of the lower back, the hips, buttocks, and thighs, and the forearm muscles. The stiff-legged version of deadlifts affects all of these muscles, plus the biceps femoris (hamstring) muscles.

This is the regular-style deadlift. The stiff-leg deadlift is merely done with the legs held straight throughout the movement.

You will eventually be able to use very heavy weights in both styles of deadlift. To keep from losing your grip, you can use what is called a *reversed grip*. In a reversed grip, one palm faces your body and the other faces away. With a regular grip, the bar tends to roll out of the fingers, because both hands are facing in the same direction. With a reversed grip, the bar can't roll out of both hands, because they are facing in different directions. As it tends to roll out of one hand it is rolling right into the other hand.

In stiff-leg deadlifts, you can attain a longer range of motion for the movement by standing either on a high wooden block or on a flat exercise bench. Ordinarily the plates of a barbell will touch the floor before you reach a fully stretched position at the bottom of the movement when doing stiff-leg deadlifts. But by standing on a block or bench, you avoid this

problem and can lower the handle of the barbell at least another 4–6 inches past the point you could normally lower it.

Hyperextensions

This movement isolates stress primarily on the *erector spinae* muscles of your lower back, with secondary emphasis placed on your hamstring muscles.

After a few training sessions, this movement will become so easy to do that you will need to add resistance. This is accomplished by holding a loose barbell plate or a light barbell behind your neck.

Good Mornings

This oddly named movement isolates stress primarily on the *erector spinae* muscles of your lower back, with secondary emphasis placed on your hamstring muscles.

With heavier weights, the barbell handle can cut into your neck. In such a case, merely pad the handle of the barbell by wrapping a towel around it. I need to pad my barbell in this manner, while Val doesn't.

Chins

This is a favorite movement among competitive bodybuilders for *latissimus dorsi* (lats) development. Secondary emphasis is placed on the biceps and forearm muscles.

There is a myriad of variations of the chin. First, you can play with grip width, moving your hands inward until they are actually touching each other, or outward as far as you can reach. You can also reverse your grip so your palms face toward your body, using a variety of grip widths. Some bodybuilders do narrow-grip chins using a triangle-shaped apparatus that allows them to use a narrow grip with their palms facing each other. This attachment is hung over a regular chinning bar. With the hands in this position, your biceps are in their strongest pulling position in relation to your lats, so you will find this triangle chin to be very effective for lat development.

Text continues on next page.

Lat Pulldowns

This is a movement very similar to chins, but of lesser intensity. It strongly stimulates the *latissimus dorsi* muscles and places secondary stress on the biceps and forearm muscles.

All of the grip variations listed for chins can also be used for lat pulldowns. Additionally, you can try a scheme of pulling one repetition down to the front of your neck, the next to the back of your neck, and so on, alternating front and back with each repetition of a set. Both chins and pulldowns build width in the lats.

Bent Rowing

This movement primarily stresses the lats, with secondary emphasis on the posterior deltoids, biceps, and forearm muscles. While chins and pulldowns build width in the lats, bent rows primarily build thickness in them.

With a barbell, you can vary your grips in the same manner as for chins and lat pulldowns. You can also do this movement with two dumbbells, which is exactly the same as a barbell bent row or with a single dumbbell held in one hand. In this latter version, your free hand should be placed on a flat exercise bench to support your torso in position during the movement. If you are rowing with your left hand, your right leg should be extended forward and bent, and your left leg should be extended to the rear and kept relatively straight. This leg position insures maximum stretch in the working back muscles at the beginning of the movement.

Another popular form of bent rowing is done with a T-bar, which is a bar about five feet long attached on one end to the floor with a hinge. Near the free end is welded a T-shaped bar across the regular bar for a handle. Then weights are placed on the free end of the bar to supply resistance of T-bar bent rowing, or simply T-bar rows. You will find that T-bar rows build a lot of thickness into the lower back muscles in addition to building latissimus dorsi muscle mass and thickness.

Seated Pulley Rowing

This movement is similar to regular bent rowing, in that it builds thickness into the lats

and places secondary emphasis on the biceps, posterior deltoids, and forearm muscles. But because of the pecular torso movement during seated pulley rowing, you also can develop a degree of latissimus dorsi width, making this an almost perfect lat movement. According to Val, this also is a perfect movement for improving a woman's posture.

Most large gyms have a special machine for seated pulley rowing, although you can improvise the movement on any floor pulley. Usually it is done with a handle similar to the chinning triangle, which allows a narrow grip with the palms facing each other.

Some bodybuilders prefer to do this movement with either a short straight bar, or with a handle that allows a much wider grip with the palms facing each other. A similar movement can be done standing upright, leaning slightly downward toward a floor pulley, and rowing with one arm at a time.

CHEST EXERCISES

Bench Press

Bench presses strongly stress the entire pectoral muscle mass and the front deltoids. Secondary stress is placed on the triceps muscles and tertiary stress on the latissimus dorsi muscles. Many bodybuilders consider bench presses to be the best, single upper body movement. In actuality, a very good bodybuilding routine could be made up of just three movements: the squat, bent row, and bench press.

With a light weight you will be able to easily get the barbell into the starting position, but very quickly you will become so strong in this movement that you will need to utilize the rack attached to a pressing bench. In such a case, load up the barbell to the poundage desired as it lies on the rack.

With extremely heavy weights, you may need to have a training partner assist you with lifting the weight on and off the rack. In any case, with heavy weights you should always have a training partner standing at the head end of your bench as a spotter. If you hold your breath

Text continues on page 77.

Shrugs

Start—Grasp a barbell with a shoulder-width grip, palms facing your body as you stand erect and the barbell resting across your upper thighs. Your arms should be held straight throughout the movement, as if they were merely cables running from your shoulders and with hooks on the end to hold the barbell. Sag your shoulders downward and forward as fully as possible.

Finish—Shrug your shoulders upward and backward as far as you can, trying to actually touch the points of your shoulders to your ears. Return to the starting point and repeat for the required number of repetitions.

Shrugs done with dumbbells.

69

Shrugs done with bench press machine.

Start—Stand erect with a narrow grip on a barbell (four to six inches between your index fingers), palms facing your body as the barbell hangs at straight arms' length across your upper thighs. You should remain standing erect throughout the movement. At all costs, avoid a back-and-forth movement of your torso as you do upright rows.

Upright Rowing

Finish—Slowly pull the barbell up along the front of your body (it should remain two to three inches away from your torso throughout its upward and downward arcs) until your hands touch the under side of your chin. Throughout the movement, your elbows should remain higher than your hands. At the top of the movement, you should roll your shoulders backward and emphasize the upward positioning of your elbows. Hold this top position for a moment to take advantage of peak contraction, then lower the barbell slowly back to the starting position. Repeat the movement for the required number of repetitions.

**Dead-
lifts**

Start—Load up a heavy barbell and have it placed on the floor. Stand up to it with your feet set at about shoulder width and your toes pointed directly ahead. Your shins should actually be touching the barbell. Bend over at the waist and grasp the barbell with a shoulder-width grip, palms facing your legs. Keeping your arms straight, bend your legs until your knees are below your hips and your hips are below your shoulders. Flatten your back and look straight ahead.

Finish—Stand erect. To do this, start the movement by slowly straightening your legs, then following through by straightening your back. Lower the weight back along the same pathway to the starting point. Repeat for the required number of repetitions.

Alternating your hands as shown will ensure a good grip.

Hyperextensions

Start—This movement can be done either on a special bench constructed for it, or lying across a table or high exercise bench. Using the special bench, merely stand within the bench facing the flat, padded board. Then lean forward onto that pad, allowing the backs of your lower legs to rest against the two pads at the rear of the machine. Adjust yourself forward so the top edge of your pelvis is in contact with the front edge of the padded board. Then place your hands behind your neck as if preparing for a sit-up and bend your torso forward so it is hanging straight down. On a bench or table, assume approximately the same position, and then have a training partner restrain your legs as you do the movement.

Finish—Simply arch backward in a sort of reverse sit-up until your torso goes slightly above an imaginary line drawn parallel to the floor. Return to the starting position and repeat the movement for the required number of repetitions.

Good Mornings

Start—Stand erect with a light barbell held behind your neck in the same position as it would be held for the start of a squat. Slightly unlock your legs and hold them unlocked throughout the movement. Doing good mornings with straight legs is an open invitation to lower back injury.

Finish—Slowly bend forward until your torso reaches a position slightly below an imaginary line drawn parallel to the floor. Return to the starting position and repeat the movement for the required number of repetitions.

Chins

Finish—Bend your arms and pull your body up to touch the chinning bar to the top part of your trapezius muscles behind your neck (for upper lat stimulation) or to the upper part of your chest in front of your neck (for lower lat stimulation). Pause for a second and then lower back to the starting position. As you are chinning up and down, you should always have your back arched. The latissimus dorsi muscles can't be fully contracted unless the back is actually arched.

Start—Stand below a chinning bar. Jump up and grasp the bar with a grip two to three inches wider on each side than your shoulders. Your palms should be facing forward. Either hang straight below the bar, or bend your knees and cross your ankles behind your legs at about knee height.

Variation of chin done with a narrow grip.

Lat Pulldowns

Finish—Perform the same type of movement as for a chin, except that you will be pulling the bar down to you rather than pulling yourself up to the bar. Touch the bar either to the back of your neck or to the front of your neck, then return it to the starting position. Repeat for the required number of repetitions.

Start—There are numerous types of lat machines, and the starting position on each one is similar to those on the others. On a Nautilus machine, you simply sit in the seat provided, buckle the seat belt across your lap to restrain your body, and then grasp the handles of the pulldown apparatus. On some freestanding lat machines and on the lat machine with a Universal Gym, grasp the handles of the machine with your palms facing forward and then sit or kneel below the pulley. In large gyms, there will be a freestanding lat machine that has a special crossbar in front of and above the seat which will restrain your knees when you are doing pulldowns with a very heavy weight. Simply sit in the seat of such a machine, grasp the pulldown handles, and wedge your knees under the restraining bar. On all variations of the lat pulldown, your arms should be straight and stretched upward as far as possible at the start of the movement.

Start—Place your feet at about shoulder width, your toes pointed slightly outward. Bend over at the waist until your torso is parallel to the floor. Unlock your legs slightly to take potential strain off your lower spine. Extend your arms below your chest and grasp a barbell with your hands set three to four inches wider on each side than shoulder width and your palms facing your legs. Your arms should be perfectly straight, and the barbell should be slightly off the floor. If it isn't off the floor in this starting position, you will have to stand on a block of wood or on a flat exercise bench to elevate your feet in relation to the floor.

Bent Rowing

Finish—Slowly bend your arms and pull the barbell directly upward until it touches the lower part of your rib cage. As you are pulling the barbell upward, your upper arms should travel outward at 45-degree angles from your torso. Pause for a second in the top position and lower the barbell back down to the stretched starting position. Repeat the movement for the required number of repetitions.

Using a dumbbell, one can concentrate on one arm at a time.

Start—Begin by grasping the handle. Then place your feet against the restraining foot bar at the front end of the bench and sit back on the bench. Your legs should be slightly unlocked throughout the movement to remove unnecessary strain from your lower spine. Straighten your arms fully and lean forward as far as you can. To achieve a full stretch in your lats, you should actually lower your head between your arms in this starting position.

Seated Pulley Rowing

Finish—Bend your arms and lean back until your torso is slightly back of a position perpendicular to the floor just as your hands contact your lower rib cage. As you are pulling the handle in to your torso, keep your upper arms down close to your sides. At the finish position, be very sure that your back is fully arched, so you can completely contract your lats. Lower back along the same path to the starting position of the movement, and repeat the exercise for the required number of repetitions.

Text continued from page 68.

while doing a very heavy bench press, you will activate the Valsalva Effect, which can cause you to black out while pressing the weight up.

A wide variety of grip widths can be used while bench pressing. The narrower the grip, the more stress is transferred to the triceps and inner edges of the pectorals. The wider the grip used, the more stress is transferred to the front deltoids and outer edges of the pectorals. Bench presses can be done in a similar manner on Nautilus and Universal Gym machines.

All forms of bench presses can also be done with dumbbells, which actually offer a superior form of muscle stimulation on the pectorals. This is provided because the hands can be brought much lower in the bottom position of a bench press when using dumbbells than when using a barbell. A barbell's handle will contact your chest and terminate the movement long before your hands would have stopped descending with a pair of dumbbells. When doing dumbbell bench presses, you can use the barbell grip with your palms facing your feet, or a grip with your palms facing inward toward each other. Each grip will stimulate your chest muscles in a slightly different manner.

Incline Press

Bench presses done lying on an incline bench transfer stress more to the upper section of the pectorals and the front deltoids. Secondary stress is placed on the triceps muscles and tertiary stress is put on the lats.

Many gyms have incline benches with racks attached to them the same as to flat benches for bench pressing, so with heavy weights you can use the rack to get the barbell into the correct starting position. Again, a variety of grip widths can be tried, and you can use dumbbells to give yourself a longer range of motion when doing incline presses. Many bodybuilders have found that they can lessen the stress on their front deltoids and place more direct stress on their upper pectorals if they do all forms of incline pressing on a 30-degree incline bench, rather than on the more commonly used 45-degree incline bench.

Decline Press

Presses done on a 15–30-degree decline bench place stress more on the lower and outer sections of the pectorals and much less on the front deltoids. Secondary stress is placed on the triceps and latissimus dorsi muscles.

As with all forms of barbell bench presses, you should try a variety of grip widths. You can also do decline presses with dumbbells, or at the bench press station of a Universal Gym.

Flyes

This movement can be done at any of the three angles at which you do bench presses: flat, incline, and decline. As such, it can stress the upper pectorals, lower and outer pectorals, or the entire pectoral mass. Secondary stress is placed on the front deltoid muscles. Flyes done on a flat or inclined bench, Val feels, are a key movement for developing breast firmness and support.

Some bodybuilders prefer doing flyes at all angles with pulleys instead of with dumbbells. Flyes can be done on a special machine called a Pec Deck as well as on a specialized Nautilus machine.

Parallel Bar Dips

This movement primarily stresses the lower and outer edges of the pectoral muscles, as well as the triceps and front deltoids.

If you lean your torso forward as you do dips, you will place more stress on your pectoral muscles. Dips in an upright position will place the most stress on your triceps and front deltoids. There are special parallel bars in many gyms that are not actually parallel, but angled inward at one end. You can do wide-grip parallel bar dips on these bars. In all forms of parallel bar dips, you will eventually find the movement exceedingly easy to perform. Then you should add resistance by tying a dumbbell around your waist and hanging it between your legs using rope or a loop of nylon webbing.

Cable Crossovers

This exercise primarily stresses the lower, outer, and inner pectorals. It is a good movement for etching in fine lines of pectoral muscle striations, which is why I always do several sets in my chest workouts at least a month before competitions.

Crossovers can be done kneeling instead of standing, and many bodybuilders prefer to do the movement in this manner. You can also do cable crossovers one arm at a time.

Pullovers

When done with straight arms, this movement primarily stretches and expands the rib cage, as well as stresses the *serratus* muscles at the sides of the rib cage. Done with arms bent, pullovers primarily stress the pectoral muscles and latissimus dorsi muscles.

When doing bent-arm pullovers, a narrow grip (four to six inches between the index fingers) is commonly used, and the pullover is started from a position with the hands resting on the chest. Then the bar is lowered in a smaller arc over the face and down behind the head, before being pulled back to the starting point. Both straight-arm and bent-arm pullovers can be done with two dumbbells, or with one dumbbell held in both hands.

One of the most common forms of pullovers among top bodybuilders is the cross-bench pullover, in which a bodybuilder lies with his or her shoulders across a bench and with hips off the bench. A dumbbell is held in both hands with the arms only slightly bent. Pullovers are done in this position to stress the pectorals and lats, as well as to enlarge the volume of the rib cage.

SHOULDER EXERCISES

Military Press

Military presses stress primarily the front head of the deltoids, the triceps, and the upper chest and back muscles.

Bending backward can make the exercise easier to do, but it can injure the lower back and robs the movement of much of its value as a shoulder developer.

As with most barbell movements, you can experiment with grip widths on military presses. This and all forms of overhead presses can be done seated on a flat exercise bench as well as standing. You will notice that you have to use less weight in a seated position than when standing, because sitting will isolate your legs from the movement.

Press Behind Neck

This is a variation on the military press that perhaps stimulates the deltoids with slightly more direct stress. Secondary emphasis is again placed on the triceps muscles.

Experiment with the grip widths discussed for military presses. Most champion bodybuilders, myself included, prefer doing presses behind neck seated. You can do presses similar to military presses and presses behind neck on a pressing machine put out by Nautilus, or on the seated press station of a Universal Gym (either facing toward or away from the weight stack).

Dumbbell Press

This movement stresses primarily the front (anterior) head of the deltoid with secondary stress on the rest of the deltoid muscle and the triceps.

The dumbbells can also be pressed alternately, with one going up as the other is coming down. And, of course, they can be done alternately with either of the two dumbbell grips previously described. You can also press a dumbbell with one arm at a time while holding on to some solid object with your free hand to brace your torso in position during the movement. Dumbbell presses—like all barbell presses—can be done seated to isolate the legs from the movement.

Dumbbell Side Laterals

This movement places stress on the front and side heads of the deltoids. Secondary stress is placed on the trapezius muscles.

Some bodybuilders like to do dumbbell side laterals one arm at a time, holding on to a solid object with their free hand to steady their bodies in position during the movement. Again, I believe this is an important factor that allows you to place more concentration on working a muscle hard.

Text continues on page 95.

Bench Press

Start—Lie back on a flat exercise bench and place your feet flat on the floor in a comfortable position to balance your body during the movement. Take a shoulder-width grip on a barbell so that your palms face your feet as you support the barbell at straight arms' length directly above your chest. Straighten your arms and lift the barbell off the rack and into position for the start of a bench press.

Finish—Bend your elbows and slowly lower the barbell straight down until it touches the lower part of your pectorals. Actually, in such a movement, the barbell will travel slightly forward as it is being lowered. As you lower and raise the barbell in a bench press, be sure that your upper arm bones travel directly out to the sides at a 90-degree angle from your torso. Once the barbell has touched your chest, push it straight back up to arms' length. Repeat the movement for the desired number of repetitions.

Incline Press

Start—Lie back on a 45-degree incline bench with the same grip on a barbell as for a bench press. Extend your arms fully so the barbell is supported at straight arms' length directly above your shoulder joints. Your arms should be perpendicular to the floor when seen from the side.

Finish—Slowly bend your elbows and lower the barbell directly downward until it touches the upper part of your chest at the base of your neck. Your upper arms should travel directly out to the sides—or perhaps even slightly to the rear—as you lower and raise the barbell in an incline press. Once the bar has touched your chest, press it back up to the starting point. Repeat the movement for the required number of repetitions.

Incline press done with dumbbells.

Decline Press

Start—Lie back on the decline board and hook your feet under the toe bar that is usually provided on such benches. If there is no toe bar, be careful to keep your knees fully bent throughout this movement, so they will prevent your body from sliding downward during this exercise. Grasp a barbell with the same grip as for a bench press and extend your arms so the barbell is supported at straight arms' length directly above your shoulder joints. Viewed from the sides, your arms would appear to be perpendicular to the floor.

Finish—Bend your elbows and slowly lower the barbell down until its handle touches the lower edge of your pectoral muscles. As you lower and raise the barbell in a decline press, be sure that your upper arm bones travel directly out to the sides. As soon as the barbell touches your chest, press it back up to the starting position. Repeat the movement for the desired number of repetitions.

Decline press done with dumbbells.

Start—Select the bench angle that stresses the section of the pectoral you prefer and lie back on it. Grasp two dumbbells in your hands and extend them directly above your chest as if preparing for a bench press. Your palms should be facing inward toward each other. Allow the dumbbells to travel toward each other until they are touching each other above the middle of your chest. Bend your arms slightly to remove stress from your elbows during the exercise.

Finish—Maintaining the degree of bend suggested for your arms, slowly lower the dumbbells directly out to the sides in semicircles to as low a position as possible. It is actually the degree to which your elbows are lowered that counts more than how low you can move the dumbbells themselves. Return the weights along the same arc to the starting point and repeat the movement for the required number of repetitions.

Flyes

Incline flyes at midpoint in movement.

Decline flyes near finish of movement.

Flyes Continued

Pec deck flyes at finish of movement.

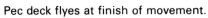

Parallel Bar Dips

Start—Grasp a pair of parallel bars with your palms facing inward and jump up on the bars so your body is supported on straight arms as illustrated. You can keep your legs straight, bend them slightly, or cross them and bend them as you did when chinning.

Finish—Bend your arms and slowly lower your body down between the bars as far as is comfortable. Your elbows should travel toward the rear as you bend your arms. Press back up to the starting position and repeat the movement for the required number of repetitions.

Start—Stand erect between the crossover pulleys and grasp a pulley handle in each hand. Your arms should be extended upward and outward in a **V** above your torso. Bend slightly forward at the waist and rotate your palms so they are facing downward.

Finish—With arms bent slightly, move the handles downward in semicircles until they touch just in front of your hips. Hold this tensed position for a few seconds. Return to the starting position and repeat for the required number of repetitions.

Pullovers

Start—Our photos illustrate the performance of straight-arm pullovers. Take a grip on a barbell and lie back on a flat bench as if preparing to do a bench press. Stiffen your arms and keep them straight throughout the movement.

Finish—Lower the barbell backward in a semicircle to a position as low behind your head as possible. As you lower the barbell, take a full breath of air. Hold that breath as you return the barbell along the same arc as it was lowered until it reaches the starting point. Exhale and repeat the movement for the required number of repetitions.

Start—Pull a barbell to the shoulders with a shoulder-width grip, so your palms are facing away from your body when the barbell is held at your shoulders. Stand erect, and be sure that you don't bend backward during the movement. Move your elbows so they are directly under the barbell handle.

Finish—Push the barbell directly upward past your face until it reaches straight arms' length directly above your head. Your upper arms should be held almost directly out to the sides as you press the weight up and down. Once the barbell has reached straight arms' length, slowly lower it back to the starting point. Repeat the movement for the required number of repetitions.

Seated military press at midpoint.

Press Behind Neck

Start—Place a barbell behind your neck as if preparing for a squat. Place your feet in a comfortable position and grasp the bar with a grip about two to three inches wider on each side than your shoulders. Stand erect throughout the movement, and move your elbows directly under the barbell handle.

Finish—Slowly press the barbell directly upward behind your head until it reaches straight arms' length above your head. Lower the barbell back to the starting position and repeat the movement for the required number of repetitions.

Dumbbell Press

Start—Pull two dumbbells up to your shoulders as if starting a military press. With dumbbells you can do your presses with your palms facing forward or with your palms facing inward.

Finish—Press the dumbbells upward simultaneously until they touch each other in the middle at straight arms' length directly over your head. Lower the weights back to your shoulders and repeat the movement for the required number of repetitions.

Dumbbell press done with alternate arms.

Dumbbell press done standing.

Dumbbell Side Laterals

Start—Grasp two dumbbells and stand erect with the dumbbells touching in front of your hips. Your palms should be facing each other and your arms should be slightly bent. Lean a little forward.

Finish—Maintaining your arms in the slightly bent position, raise the dumbbells in semicircles directly out to the sides until your arms reach an imaginary line drawn parallel to the floor. At the top position, rotate your hands so the front edges of the dumbbells are below the back edges. This small rotation puts maximum stress on the side head of your deltoid. Lower the dumbbells back to the starting position and repeat the movement for the required number of repetitions.

One-arm side lateral, start.

One-arm side lateral, finish.

Bent Laterals

Start—Grasp two dumbbells and bend over until your torso is parallel to the floor. Unlock your knees slightly to take strain off your lower back during the movement. Your arms should be hanging straight down from your shoulders and your palms should be facing toward each other. Bend your arms slightly and press the dumbbells together.

Finish—Slowly raise the dumbbells directly out to the sides and upward in semicircles until your arms are above an imaginary line drawn parallel to the floor. Pause in the top position for a moment and then lower the weights back down to the starting point. Repeat the movement for the required number of repetitions.

Seated bent lateral, finish.

Front Raises

Start—We will describe a front raise with a barbell, and you can then generalize that description for use with dumbbells or cables. Take a shoulder-width grip on a barbell so your palms are facing your body as the barbell rests across your upper thighs while you are standing erect. Stiffen your arms.

Front Raises Continued

Finish—Keeping your arms and body stiff, slowly raise the barbell forward and upward in a semicircle from your thighs until it reaches an imaginary line drawn parallel to the floor. Hold this top position for a moment and then lower the barbell back along the same arc to the starting point. Repeat the movement for the required number of repetitions.

Alternate front raises with dumbbells.

Bent Laterals

This movement places direct stress on the rear head of the deltoid. Secondary stress is placed on all of the upper back muscles.

This movement is often done seated at the end of a flat exercise bench with the front of the torso resting along the tops of the thighs. Some bodybuilders prefer doing bent laterals with cables rather than with dumbbells.

Front Raises

Whether done with a barbell, cable, two dumbbells, or one dumbbell, this movement isolates stress on the anterior (front) head of the deltoid.

Many bodybuilders prefer doing front raises (or front laterals) with two dumbbells, raising the bells alternately. When you raise a dumbbell upward in this movement, you will find you receive superior front deltoid stimulation if you raise it up the midline of your body, or—if possible—actually past the midline of your body. You can also do front raises with a single dumbbell held in both hands, with a pulley one arm at a time, or with a pulley and both arms at a time.

Cable Side Laterals

This movement is excellent for stimulating the medial (side) head of the deltoid. In the past year, I added another inch to my shoulder width primarily with this exercise.

You can receive stimulation from a slightly different angle if you pass the cable behind your body during this movement, rather than in front of your body.

ARM EXERCISES

Barbell Curl

This exercise places direct stress on the biceps muscles and secondary stress on the muscles of the inner forearms.

If you have trouble with torso movement during the exercise, you can do barbell curls with your back pressed against a wall or post. This will quite effectively eliminate all torso

movement when doing any form of curls. You should periodically experiment with various grip widths on all barbell curls. Each slight change in grip width will place a different stress on the muscles on the front of your upper arms. You can also use an "EZ-curl" bar instead of a straight bar for barbell curls.

Dumbbell Curl

This exercise, like the barbell curl, places direct stress on the biceps muscles and secondary stress on the muscles of the inner forearms.

As you curl, your wrists should rotate so your palms are facing upward at the top position of the curl. Taking your right hand as an example, your thumb will move clockwise during the curl. This twisting of the wrist is called *supination,* and it gives the biceps a better quality of stress than you can receive from barbell curls.

As with dumbbell presses, dumbbell curls are often done alternately, with one hand going upward as the other hand descends. You can also do all forms of standing dumbbell curls seated at the end of a flat exercise bench to isolate your legs from the movement.

Incline Curl

This movement puts very strong stress on the biceps muscles and less stress on the muscles on the insides of your forearms.

This movement was popularized by the legendary Steve Reeves, who nailed a crossbar under his bench to further restrain his upper arms during the movement. This was a crude forerunner of the preacher bench (see the next exercise). I have a favorite variation of the incline curl in which I lie facedown, rather than faceup, on the bench and curl the dumbbells upward from this position. My form of doing incline curls results in a superior *peak contraction* in my biceps at the top of each repetition of the movement.

Preacher Curl

This movement was popularized by Larry Scott, the first Mr. Olympia winner. It builds roundness in the biceps, and particularly stimulates the lower part of the biceps muscles.

This movement can be done with two dumbbells simultaneously, or with one dumbbell at a time. When using one dumbbell at a time, you can run your arm down an incline bench.

Concentration Curl

This exercise builds the peak of the biceps muscle. If you have the potential for building a high biceps peak, this movement will bring out that peak.

This movement is occasionally done with a dumbbell while standing almost erect and hanging the curling arm straight downward. You can also use a barbell to do concentration curls with both hands by bending over at the waist until your torso is parallel to the floor. Then hang both arms directly downward and curl from that position. Usually barbell concentration curls are done with a narrow grip (about four or five inches between your little fingers).

Cable Pushdown

This exercise stresses the whole of the triceps muscle, but particularly the outer head of the triceps.

This exercise can be done one hand at a time with a loop handle and/or with a reversed grip. Various handles can be used for doing pushdowns—a regular lat bar, a short angled handle, a short straight handle, a rope handle, and a loop handle.

Barbell Triceps Extension

Barbell triceps extensions stress the whole of the triceps muscle, but particularly the large inner head of the triceps.

This exercise can be done seated at the end of a flat bench, lying on a flat bench, lying on an incline bench, or lying on a decline bench. All of these variations will give a slightly different feel to the movement. In all variations, the key to effectively using the movement is to restrain the movement of your upper arms.

Dumbbell Triceps Extension

This exercise is very similar in emphasis to barbell triceps extensions.

This exercise can be done seated or lying on variously angled exercise benches. It can be done with two dumbbells held in your hands, or with a single dumbbell held in one hand.

Triceps Pushups

This movement places stress on the whole of the triceps muscle, but particularly on the outer head of the triceps.

This exercise is an excellent one for a *finishing pump* in your triceps. Once it becomes easy to do triceps pushups with just your body weight, add resistance to the movement by holding a barbell plate in the angle between your torso and thighs.

Dumbbell Kickbacks

This exercise stresses the entire triceps muscle mass. It is particularly effective as a peak contraction movement, which will be discussed in detail in Chapter 5.

This movement can be done with two dumbbells, extending both arms to the rear.

Reverse Curls

Reverse curls stress the biceps, the *brachialis* muscle lying under the biceps, and the upper section of your forearms.

Although some bodybuilders do this movement with their wrists flexed, we feel it is best to do reverse curls with the wrists held straight. For variety, you can do this movement with a narrow grip.

Barbell Wrist Curls

This exercise stresses all of the muscles of the forearms.

With your palms facing upward during the exercise, you will be stressing the muscles on the inner sides of your forearms. To stress the outer sides of your forearms, simply turn your palms downward during the movement. You will find you can use about half as much weight with your palms turned downward as with them turned upward. To make this movement more strict, you can run your arms along a flat exercise bench, rather than down your thighs.

Dumbbell Wrist Curls

This exercise also stresses all of the muscles of the forearms.

For greater concentration, you can do dumbbell wrist curls one arm at a time. Whether using one arm or two for the movement, you also can run your arms along the top of a flat exercise bench. As with barbell wrist curls, having your palms up during the movement stresses the inner sections of your forearms, while having your palms down stresses the outer part of your forearm musculature.

Cable Side Laterals

Start—Cable side laterals are normally done one arm at a time. Stand with your left side toward a floor pulley. Your left foot should be about two to three feet away from the pulley and your feet should be set a comfortable distance apart. Grasp the handle of the floor pulley in your right hand so your arm and the pulley cable run across the front of your body during the movement. Place your left hand on your hip and allow your right hand to travel as far as possible toward the pulley. Bend your right arm slightly.

Finish—Raise the handle outward and upward to the side in a semicircle until your hand is above an imaginary line drawn parallel to the floor. As you raise the handle, your hand should also travel slightly out to the front as well as to the side. Hold the top position for a moment and then lower the weight back to the starting point. Repeat the movement for the required number of repetitions.

Cable Side Laterals Continued

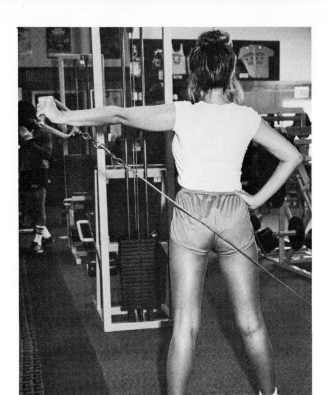

Cable side lateral with cable behind body.

Barbell Curl

Start—Stand erect with a shoulder-width grip on a barbell, so your palms are facing away from your body as the barbell rests across your upper thighs. Press your upper arms in against the sides of your torso and keep them there throughout the exercise. Fully straighten your arms, and stiffen your torso so it doesn't move back and forth during the exercise.

Finish—Move only your forearms and elbows to curl the barbell in a semicircle from your thighs to your chin. As you curl the weight upward, you can slowly flex your wrists. Return the weight down along its upward arc until it is back at the starting position. Repeat the barbell curl for the desired number of repetitions.

Dumbbell Curl

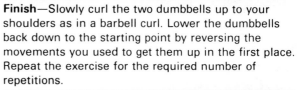

Start—Stand erect as in a barbell curl, but hold two dumbbells down at the sides of your hips with your palms facing inward toward each other.

Finish—Slowly curl the two dumbbells up to your shoulders as in a barbell curl. Lower the dumbbells back down to the starting point by reversing the movements you used to get them up in the first place. Repeat the exercise for the required number of repetitions.

Alternate dumbbell curls.

Seated dumbbell curls.

Start—Grasp two dumbbells in your hands and lie back on a 45-degree incline bench so your arms are hanging straight down from your shoulders. Your palms should be facing inward at the start of the exercise, so you can supinate your hands during the movement.

Finish—Being sure to keep your upper arms from moving and to supinate your hands during the movement, slowly curl both dumbbells up to your shoulders. Lower them back to the starting point and repeat for the desired number of repetitions.

Incline Curl

Variation of incline curl done face down.

100

Preacher Curl—Starts

Start—Take an under-grip on a barbell with your hands set slightly wider than shoulder width. Lean over a preacher bench and run your arms down the angled pad. Your armpits should be against the top edge of the pad. Straighten your arms fully.

Finish—Keeping your upper arms motionless on the bench, slowly curl the barbell up to your neck. Return it slowly to the starting position and repeat for the required number of repetitions.

Preacher Curl— Finishes

102

Alternate preacher curl.

Concentration Curl

Start—Sit at the end of a flat exercise bench. Spread your feet wide enough to create a 90-degree angle between your thighs. Grasp a dumbbell in your left hand and bend over enough to be able to place your left triceps against the inside of your left thigh near your knee. You can rest your right hand on your right leg or brace it behind your left arm.

Finish—Keeping your upper arm motionless, curl the dumbbell from a position with your arm straight until your arm is fully flexed. Return the weight to the starting point and repeat the movement for the required number of repetitions.

Concentration Curl Continued

Concentration curl done with barbell.

Cable Pulldowns

Start—Take a narrow over-grip in the middle of the lat machine handle. Press your upper arms close to your sides and fully bend your arms, so the handle is up under your chin.

Finish—Keeping your upper arms motionless, slowly straighten your arms completely. Return to the starting position and repeat.

Start—Grasp a barbell in the middle of its handle with a narrow over-grip. Stand erect and push the barbell up to straight arms' length overhead. Hold your upper arms motionless throughout the movement. They should be right up next to your head.

Finish—Moving just your forearms, lower the barbell slowly in a semicircle from the starting position until it touches the back of your neck. Return the weight back along this same arc to the starting point. Repeat the movement for the required number of repetitions.

Barbell Triceps Extension

Seated barbell triceps extension.

Lying barbell triceps extension.

Decline barbell triceps extension.

Barbell Triceps Extension Continued

Incline barbell triceps extension.

Dumbbell Triceps Extension

Start—Hold a single dumbbell in both hands in the same position as for the start of barbell triceps extensions. Your grip on the dumbbell should be such that the handle hangs vertically and your palms should overlap each other, the upper one resting against the inner side of the dumbbell plates.

Finish—Restraining your upper arms during the movement, bend your elbows and lower the dumbbell in a semicircle from the starting point until it touches your upper back and your elbows are fully bent. Return the weight along the same arc to the starting point and repeat the movement for the desired number of repetitions.

Triceps extension done with two dumbbells.

Triceps extension done with alternate arms.

Triceps
Push-Ups

Start—You will need two flat exercise benches placed parallel to each other and about three feet apart to do this movement. Place your heels on one bench and your hands on the other. Your hands should be placed close together on the bench with your fingers pointed toward your toes. Your torso should make a right angle with your legs, which are held straight throughout the movement.

Finish—Slowly bend your arms as fully as possible, lowering your body between the two benches. Press back to the starting position and repeat the movement for the required number of repetitions.

Start—Bend over at the waist until your torso is parallel to the floor. Place your right hand on a flat exercise bench to maintain this torso position throughout the movement. Grasp a light dumbbell in your left hand and press your upper arm in against your side. Hold your arm in this position throughout the movement. You should turn your wrist so your palm faces toward the midline of your body.

Finish—Beginning with your forearm perpendicular to the floor, fully straighten your arm. Hold this straight position for a count of two, then lower the weight back to the starting point. Repeat for the desired number of repetitions. Do an equal amount of work for your right arm.

Dumbbell Kickbacks

Dumbbell kickback done with two dumbbells.

Start—Take a shoulder-width over-grip on a barbell. Stand erect with your arms straight and the barbell resting across your upper thighs. Press your upper arms against the sides of your body and keep them in this position throughout the movement.

Finish—Moving just your forearms, curl the barbell in a semicircle from your thighs to your chin. Lower it back along the same arc to the starting point and repeat the movement for the required number of repetitions.

Reverse curl done with narrow-grip bar.

Reverse Curls

**Barbell
Wrist
Curls**

Start—Take a shoulder-width under-grip on a barbell. Sit at the end of a flat exercise bench and place your feet at shoulder width. Run your forearms down your thighs, so your wrists hang off the edges of your knees.

Finish—Sag your hands as far downward as possible. Then slowly curl the barbell in a small semicircle upward until your wrists are fully flexed. Lower back to the starting point and repeat the movement for the required number of repetitions.

Barbell wrist curl done with reversed grip.

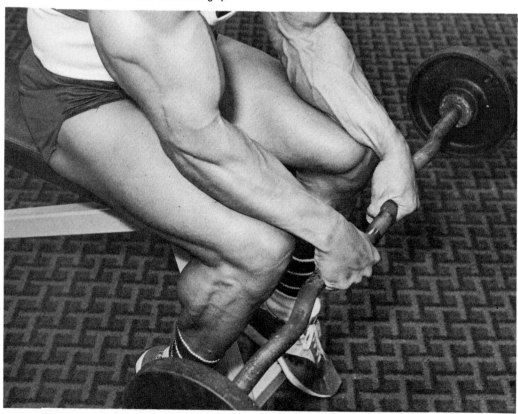

Start—Except that you will be holding two dumbbells in your hands, the starting position for the movement is the same as for barbell wrist curls.

Finish—This is also identical to the movement for barbell wrist curls.

Dumbbell Wrist Curls

Wrist curl done with one arm.

WHAT'S NEXT?

In the next chapter, we will combine all of these weight training exercises into a wide variety of routines that you can begin using right away in an effort to reach your weight training and bodybuilding goals.

4
Weight Training Exercise Routines

After reading an introduction to this book and the two lengthy chapters on basic training techniques and weight training exercises, we're sure you are overjoyed finally to get down to doing a weight training workout. In this chapter there are nine such training programs presented. They are of graduated difficulty, and several of the intermediate and advanced training programs are keyed specifically toward achieving the various goals of weight training we explained in Chapter 1 (weight gain, weight loss, body toning, etc.).

It is obvious to us that many of our readers will already have varying degrees of weight training experience behind them. Such men and women will need to choose the training routines in this chapter according to their degree of experience. Therefore, we offer the following guidelines for choosing the correct training level for yourself. In the chart below, the figures of "months trained" are assumed to encompass various lengths of *steady* training; if you have trained sporadically with weights over the years, count only the most recent stretch of uninterrupted training.

When adopting one of these routines following a layoff from weight training, be sure to take appropriate break-in measures as outlined in Chapter 2. If you have been on a layoff lasting more than a week, you will experience very severe muscle soreness if you attempt to resume training on a full-scale workout. You will be far more comfortable if you use two to three weeks to gradually break in to a full routine after any extended weight training layoff.

Months Trained	Appropriate Level
0–1½	First routine—beginning level.
1½–3	Second routine—beginning level.
3–4½	Third routine—beginning level.
4½–8	Any routine—intermediate level.
8–12	The four-day split routine—advanced level.
12–18	The five-day split routine—advanced level.
18–24	The six-day split routine (each body part twice per week)—advanced level.
24+	The six-day split routine (each body part three times per week)—advanced level.

BEGINNING ROUTINES

In this section we have outlined three workout routines of progressively greater training intensity and difficulty. Each is a general routine designed to condition your body for much more intense, specialized weight workouts at the intermediate and advanced training levels.

These beginning routines are full-body workouts that should be undertaken on three nonconsecutive days each week; most commonly on Mondays, Wednesdays, and Fridays as was explained in detail in Chapter 2. Also—as mentioned in Chapter 2 under the heading "How Much Weight?"—we will suggest starting poundages for each exercise in terms of a percentage of your body weight, but for only the first routine in this section. After six weeks of steady training on that workout schedule, you should be able to judge the appropriate poundage to use for every exercise in each subsequent routine.

Remember to follow the break-in procedures outlined in Chapter 2 for this routine. If you've never before touched a weight, you should use two to three weeks to break gradually and easily into the full workout.

This and every routine that we suggest in this book is specifically designed to offer exercise for every muscle group in the body, except for the neck. We firmly believe in doing routines with a balance of exercises for all body parts, because the human body—like a steel chain—is only as strong as its weakest link.

Very few men or women other than male football players (who participate in a sport placing a premium on powerful neck development) will ever need to do direct exercise to enlarge and strengthen their neck muscles. The neck grows very easily in size and will remain in proportion to the rest of the body simply due to the growth stimulus it is provided indirectly by upper back and shoulder movements and upright rows, dumbbell presses, and barbell presses.

Level One (weeks 1–6)

Exercise	Sets	Reps	% Men	% Women
1. Sit-Ups	1	20–50	——	——
2. Squats	3	8–12	40%	30%
3. Barbell Bent Rowing	3	8–12	35%	25%
4. Upright Rowing	2	8–12	30%	20%
5. Bench Press	3	8–12	35%	25%
6. Military Press	2	8–12	30%	20%
7. Barbell Curl	2	8–12	25%	15%
8. Cable Pushdowns	2	8–12	20%	10%
9. Barbell Wrist Curl	3	15–20	20%	10%
10. Standing Calf Machine	3	15–20	50%	40%

Level Two (weeks 7–12)

Exercise	Sets	Reps
1. Leg Raises	1–2	25–50
2. Seated Twisting	1–2	50–100
3. Squats	3	8–12
4. Leg Extension	2	8–12
5. Leg Curl	2	8–12
6. Hyperextensions	1	10–15
7. Barbell Shrugs	2	10–15
8. Seated Pulley Rowing	3	8–12
9. Bench Press	3	6–10
10. Incline Barbell Press	2	6–10
11. Press Behind Neck	2	6–10
12. Dumbbell Side Laterals	2	8–12
13. Dumbbell Curl	2	8–12
14. Concentration Curl	2	8–12
15. Cable Pushdown	2	8–12
16. Lying Barbell Triceps Extension	2	8–12
17. Barbell Wrist Curl	2	15–20
18. Barbell Reverse Wrist Curl	2	15–20
19. Barbell Calf Raise	2–3	15–20
20. Seated Calf Machine	2	15–20

Level Three (weeks 13–18)

Exercise	Sets	Reps
1. Knee-Ups	2–3	25–50
2. Side Bends	2–3	50–100
3. Bench Squats	4	8–12
4. Lunges	3	8–12
5. Leg Curls	3	8–12
6. Stiff-Leg Deadlift	2	10–15
7. Dumbbell Shrugs	3	10–15
8. Lat Pulldowns	4	8–12
9. Incline Dumbbell Press	3	6–10
10. Decline Barbell Press	2	8–12
11. Dumbbell Press	2	6–10
12. Dumbbell Side Laterals	2	8–12
13. Bent Laterals	2	8–12
14. Incline Curl	2–3	8–12
15. Preacher Curl	2	8–12
16. Dumbbell Triceps Extension	3	8–12
17. Dumbbell Kickbacks	2	8–12
18. Reverse Curl	2	8–12
19. Dumbbell Wrist Curl	2	15–20
20. Dumbbell Reverse Wrist Curl	2	15–20
21. Donkey Calf Raise	3	15–20
22. Toe Press	2–3	15–20

INTERMEDIATE ROUTINES

At the intermediate level you can begin to do specialized routines to accelerate your progress toward one of the goals outlined in Chapter 1. In this section we will present specialized routines for five purposes: (1) gaining weight; (2) losing weight; (3) specializing in acquiring exceptional strength; (4) men's and women's body toning and health improvement; and (5) men's and women's bodybuilding.

The men's and women's bodybuilding routine is appropriate for sports improvement as well, although training programs individualized for a wide variety of sports are presented in two fine books, *Complete Weight Training Book* by Bill Reynolds and *Gold's Gym Book of Strength Training* by Ken Sprague. We recommend that you eventually follow a routine outlined in one of these books that's specially tailored to improve your sports performance in your favorite athletic activity.

Gaining Weight

Gaining muscle mass and losing weight (discussed in detail in the next section of this chapter) require a combination of specialized diet and specialized training. More than 50% of the letters we receive and of the questions we field at our seminars come from underweight men and women who fervently want to gain body weight and achieve a more normal physical appearance.

The secret to gaining weight is to train heavily on basic exercises and do short workouts that won't overtax the body's recuperative ability. The accent must always be on using maximum training poundages (always with good exercise form), because there is a direct relationship between the heaviness of the weights you use in your exercises and the size of your muscles. The heavier the weights you use, the larger your muscles will be. And the larger your muscles, the heavier your body weight and the more normal your appearance. (Remember, a woman's added muscle mass will appear on her body as feminine curves.)

Using the guidelines we have just set forth for weight-gain training, here is a sample weight

training program you can use three nonconsecutive days per week:

Weight Gaining

Exercise	Sets	Reps
1. Sit-Ups	2–3	25–50
2. Squats	5	4–12*
3. Barbell Bent Rowing	5	4–12*
4. Bench Press	5	4–12*
5. Good Mornings	1–2	10–15
6. Upright Rowing	1–2	8–12
7. Barbell Curls	1–2	8–12
8. Lying Barbell Triceps Extension	1–2	8–12
9. Barbell Wrist Curls	1–2	15–20
10. Barbell Reverse Wrist Curls	1–2	15–20
11. Standing Calf Machine	1–2	15–20
12. Seated Calf Machine	1–2	15–20

*Pyramid weights and reps for these exercises.

Pyramidding. On the starred (*) exercises, your first set should be done for 12 reps with a moderate poundage. For your second set, add 10–20 pounds and do 10 reps, then add more weight and do 8 reps, add more weight and do 6 reps, and finally add more weight and do 4 reps. This scheme of raising the weight and lowering the number of reps to be done on each succeeding set is called *pyramidding*. It is a good technique for gaining strength and hence adding muscle mass to the body in any exercise.

While the foregoing weight training routine will stimulate growth in your muscle mass, it only goes halfway in helping you gain weight at optimum speed. Optimally, the weight workout must be combined with a diet that's high in calories and that promotes maximum protein assimilation (since protein is necessary for building large muscles).

The key to eating like this is to consume five to seven small, snack-like meals each day, rather than two or three huge feasts a day. A man's body can normally digest and assimilate a maximum of 30 grams of protein per feeding, a woman's body a maximum of 25 grams of protein each meal. Therefore, if you eat numerous small, protein-rich meals each day your body will use more total protein every day—and hence will add muscle mass at a faster pace—than it can when you eat larger and less frequent meals.

Using these guidelines, here is a typical daily menu for a man or woman interested in gaining weight:

Meal One (8:00 a.m.)—cheese omelet, full-fat raw milk, and one multipack of vitamins and minerals.

Meal Two (10:00 a.m.)—high-protein milkshake: eight to ten ounces of raw milk, one to two heaping tablespoons of 90% milk-and-egg protein powder, and flavorings, all mixed in a blender.

Meal Three (12:00 p.m.)—tuna salad, fruit, raw milk, and one multipack.

Meal Four (2:00 p.m.)—another high-protein milkshake.

Meal Five (4:00 p.m.)—meat or poultry, baked potato, raw milk, and one multipack.

Meal Six (6:00 p.m.)—high-protein milkshake.

Meal Seven (8:00 p.m.)—same as Meal Five.

Milk is a key weight-gaining food, because it is easy to consume and is high in both protein and calories. But some men and women—more men than women, more blacks than whites, more older individuals than younger ones—are allergic to milk. More specifically, their stomachs don't have the enzyme (*lactase*) necessary to digest the sugar (*lactose*) in milk. If you have a milk allergy it will present itself as post-meal bloating, increased flatulence, and sometimes post-meal drowsiness. With such an allergy, you will still be able to consume milk products like hard cheeses, which have had the lactose removed in processing. Virtually everyone with a milk allergy is allergic only to the lactose in the milk, not to any of milk's other nutrients.

Even eating six to seven small meals a day might not help you to gain weight, particularly if your digestive efficiency is poor. If your stomach doesn't produce a normal flow of digestive acids and enzymes, you'll get little value from the food you eat. Hence, it will be difficult to put on body weight.

Underpar digestive efficiency can be improved by taking hydrochloric acid capsules and digestive enzyme tablets each time you eat. Both of these digestive aids are available in health food stores, and regular use of hydrochloric acid and digestive enzymes (principally *papain*, the enzyme found in pineapples) will give you the digestive efficiency that Nature failed to provide to you. With better digestive efficiency, more of the food you eat can be used to add muscle mass to your body and you will be able to gain weight at a faster rate.

Losing Weight

A large proportion of questions that we receive from men and women who are not seeking to gain weight invariably come from individuals trying to slim down and lose weight. Again, a combination of specialized diet and specialized training will help you to knock off all of the body fat you desire, *if* you apply the diet and exercise programs diligently. Such a combination has worked perfectly for Val, who had a few pounds of fat to lose when she started bodybuilding training.

Any human being stores excess calories that he or she consumes as body fat in Nature's defense against famine and starvation. But America is a land of plenty and we needn't store fat, because the chance of starving is minimal. Still, more than 40% of all Americans have systematically overeaten to such an extent that they are noticeably obese.

To lose body fat, you simply need to reverse the trend that made you overweight to start with: eating more calories than your body could expend each day. Thus, you must begin to systematically undereat: take in less calories each day than your body requires to fulfill its energy needs, thus forcing your body to draw on its stored fat reserves to make up the caloric deficit. This is traditionally done by going on a low-calorie diet.

Val and Boyer review one of their nutrition articles before preparing dinner.

Dieting by itself will effectively reduce your body fat levels, but it won't do the job as quickly and esthetically by itself as it will in combination with regular exercise. Exercise, particularly aerobic activity, increases the caloric deficit established with a diet by increasing the number of calories your body requires to meet its energy needs. And the exercise you receive from weight training will keep your muscle and skin in good tone, eliminating the problem of having the type of unsightly, hanging flab that accompanies diet-only, weight reduction programs.

Personally, we don't use or recommend low-carbohydrate diets, because they are so nutritionally unbalanced that they can actually cause harm to your body. Deprived of its normal supplies of blood sugar, your brain can react negatively. You can become lethargic, dull-witted, and emotionally depressed quite easily when your brain is deprived of blood sugar.

The easiest type of diet to follow—as well as the weight reduction regimen that most promotes optimum health—is simply a nutritionally balanced diet with a restricted caloric in-

take. Additionally, this caloric restriction should be undertaken gradually and progressively, so your body can adapt comfortably to each new reduction in total caloric intake without undue strain.

As mentioned in the section in Chapter 2 entitled "Basic Diet Tips," it is easiest to reduce the total number of calories in your diet by reducing the amount of fat you consume. Since one gram of fat yields nine calories of energy when metabolized in your body, versus four calories per gram each of protein and carbohydrate, dietetic fat reduction makes good sense when limiting total caloric intake.

High-fat foods include all oils, butter, beef, pork, ham, bacon, eggs, full-fat milk products, corn, some nuts, some seeds, and some grains. Low-fat foods include all fresh fruits, fresh vegetables, fish, and poultry (but be sure to remove the fatty skin of chicken and turkey before cooking).

Begin your weight reduction diet by taking full stock of how you actually eat today. We suggest recording all of the foods, including good estimates of the quantities of each food you consume, that you eat for one week in a food diary. Then analyze your diary to see patterns developing. Perhaps you tend to eat junk food every fourth day, or you eat a lot of high-fat cheeses. Actually sit down with your one-week food diary and plan where to make minor cuts in the amounts of fat you eat in a week, as well as in amounts of refined white sugar and white flour. Make these reductions in small, gradual increments, however, or it will become easy to fall off the dieting wagon. Judge how much to cut out by your late-afternoon energy levels. You should always try to be *slightly* drained of energy, because that's a sure sign that you're in a negative caloric balance.

Typical further caloric reductions would consist of eating a couple of extra fish or chicken meals each week, inserting them in your overall diet where you would ordinarily have eaten beef. If you still have junk food cravings, satiate them by eating a large piece of watermelon, a couple baskets of strawberries, or some other type of sweet fruit. After a month of such gradual and progressive caloric intake reductions—plus regular exercise—you'll notice a significant dip in your body fat levels. And you will have achieved it on an essentially painless diet!

As previously mentioned, a weight-loss exercise program should combine aerobic activity with weight training. To burn up extra calories, you should try to schedule approximately 30 minutes of aerobic exercise almost daily, if not actually on a daily basis. Keeping in mind that you will lose one pound of body fat for each 3500 calories you burn off, here is a brief list of the approximate number of calories you can expend with 30 minutes of exercise in several popular physical activities:

Aerobic Activity	Calories Expended
1. Running (10 mph)	450
2. Bicycling (20 mph)	330
3. Handball or Racquetball	300
4. Swimming (2½ mph)	275
5. Walking (1 mph)	100

A weight training program for fat loss should include exercises for all of the body's muscle groups. Moderate weights should be used and relatively high repetitions (15–20) should be done for each exercise. Here is a good weight training program you can follow three nonconsecutive days per week to tone your muscles and skin while on a weight-loss program:

Weight Loss Training

Exercise	Sets	Reps
1. Sit-Ups	2–3	25–50
2. Leg Raises	2–3	25–50
3. Side Bends	2–3	50–100
4. Seated Twisting	2–3	50–100
5. Squats	3	15–20
6. Lunges	2	15–20
7. Leg Extensions	2	15–20
8. Leg Curls	2	15–20
9. Hyperextensions	2–3	15–20
10. Upright Rowing	2–3	15–20
11. Lat Pulldown	2–3	15–20
12. Dumbbell Bent Rowing	2–3	15–20
13. Incline Dumbbell Press	2–3	15–20
14. Decline Flyes	2–3	15–20
15. Cable Crossovers	2–3	15–20
16. Barbell Front Raise	2–3	15–20
17. Cable Side Laterals	2	15–20
18. Bent Laterals	2	15–20
19. Incline Curl	2	15–20
20. Barbell Curl	2	15–20
21. Dumbbell Triceps Extension	2	15–20
22. Triceps Pushups	2	15–20
23. Reverse Curl	2	15–20
24. Barbell Wrist Curl	2	20–30
25. Barbell Reverse Wrist Curl	2	20–30
26. Standing Calf Machine	1–2	20–30
27. Seated Calf Machine	1–2	20–30
28. One-Leg Toe Raise	1–2	20–30

This program includes a wide variety of exercises which will thoroughly stimulate every muscle group from a variety of angles. And there are a great number of total reps to be done, which can give you an aerobic effect if you hold your rest intervals to 30 seconds or less.

The foregoing weight reduction, weight training routine includes more than the usual amount of abdominal work than we recommend. Don't let this seduce you into accepting the myth that you can *spot reduce,* however. Doing a great number of exercises for any body part (e.g., your abdomen or hips) will *not* lead to a quick fat loss in that area. At best, adopting such a training philosophy will merely tone the muscles underlying the area.

Every human being loses fat all over his or her body when creating a caloric deficit by dieting and exercising. No one loses fat just in one area. There are, however, individual patterns of fat accumulation and loss which vary from man to man, and from woman to woman. You will tend to lose fat first in certain areas and faster in some areas than in others. When you gain back fat after falling off a diet you will invariably put it on more quickly in some areas than in others.

Strength Specialization

To develop great strength you must train your mind and your body to accept your ability to handle very heavy weights. This is most efficiently done by concentrating your workouts on basic exercises and doing a relatively high number of sets (4–6) of relatively low repetitions (1–5) for each basic exercise.

Following the above philosophies, here is a strength building routine you can use on three nonconsecutive training days each week:

Once each two weeks—and on a rotating basis—the final set of each exercise should be done with a weight heavy enough to elicit 100% mental and muscular effort to complete it successfully.

Men's and Women's Body Toning

At the intermediate training level, body-toning weight workouts for both men and women will merely be progressions of intensity past the Level Three beginners' workout. You can, however, begin to direct specialized attention at a weak or poorly toned body part at this training level. Such specialized attention will consist of simply doing extra sets and additional exercises for lagging body parts.

Assuming that your thigh development and muscle tone are lagging behind the rest of your body, we present a body-toning weight workout any man or woman can use three days per week to stress that area on page 123.

If you faithfully follow this routine for 4–6 weeks, you will notice improved overall body tone, particularly in your thighs. Of course you can specialize on any other body part you wish to improve more quickly than the rest of your body simply by doing a greater number of total sets for it.

Men's and Women's Bodybuilding

The main goal of an intermediate male or female bodybuilder should be to continue increasing the overall intensity of each workout in order to continue adding muscle mass all over the body. Such mass should be added proportionately, however, and by the time you have been training steadily for 4–6 months you will be able to notice lagging muscle groups. Spe-

Strength Building Workout

Exercise	Sets	Reps	Exercise	Sets	Reps
1. Sit-Ups	2–3	25–50	5. Deadlifts	6	6-5-4-3-2-1*
2. Hyperextensions	1	15–20	6. Barbell Bent Rowing	4	6-5-4-4*
3. Squats	6	6-5-4-3-2-1*	7. Barbell Curl	3	6-5-4*
4. Bench Presses	6	6-5-4-3-2-1*	8. Standing Calf Machine	5	12-10-8-6-5*
*Pyramid weights and reps for these exercises.					

cialize on such weak muscle groups by training them more intensely and with more sets, plus work them into the start of your training session when your physical and mental energies are highest.

At the intermediate level, you will probably experience your fastest growing rates in major muscle groups when doing 4–8 reps per set with heavy weights and using strict form. Your calves, abdominals, and forearms will respond best to reps in the range of 10–15.

Assuming that you need to specialize on the pectoral muscles of your chest, in the chart below we present a good men's and women's intermediate bodybuilding program that you can use three nonconsecutive days each week.

Some champion bodybuilders and other bodybuilding authorities would consider this routine to be overly long. Our feeling about this is that champion bodybuilders—for the most part—do long and involved training routines, so you should get used to them early in your

Body Toning Workout
(thigh specialization)

Exercise	Sets	Reps
1. Hanging Frog Kicks	2–3	10–15
2. Seated Twisting	2–3	50–100
3. Squat	3	10–15
4. Hack Squat	2–3	10–15
5. Lunges	2–3	10–15
6. Leg Extension	2–3	10–15
7. Leg Curl	4–5	10–15
8. Stiff-Leg Deadlift	1	15–20
9. Dumbbell Shrugs	1–2	10–15
10. Seated Pulley Rowing	3–4	8–12
11. Incline Barbell Press	3–4	6–10
12. Flat-Bench Flyes	2–3	8–12
13. Alternate Dumbbell Press	2–3	6–10
14. Dumbbell Side Laterals	2	8–12
15. Bent Laterals	2	8–12
16. Alternate Dumbbell Curl	2–3	8–12
17. Preacher Curls	2	8–12
18. Pulley Pushdown	2–3	8–12
19. Dumbbell Kickbacks	2	8–12
20. Reverse Curl	2	8–12
21. Dumbbell Wrist Curl	2	15–20
22. Dumbbell Reverse Wrist Curl	2	15–20
23. Donkey Calf Raise	2	15–20
24. Seated Calf Machine	2	15–20
25. Toe Press	1	15–20

Bodybuilding Workout

Exercise	Sets	Reps
1. Incline Sit-Ups	2–3	15–25
2. Hanging Frog Kicks	2–3	15–25
3. Side Bends	2–3	50–100
4. Parallel Bar Dips	4	6–8
5. Incline Dumbbell Press	3	6–8
6. Barbell Bench Press	3	6–8
7. Flat-Bench Flyes	2–3	8–10
8. Dumbbell Pullovers	2–3	8–10
9. Dumbbell Press	3	4–6
10. Upright Rowing	2–3	6–8
11. Bent Laterals	2–3	6–8
12. Chins	3	6–8
13. Dumbbell Bent Rowing	3	6–8
14. Good Mornings	1–2	10–12
15. Squats	4–5	6–10
16. Leg Extensions	3	8–10
17. Leg Curl	4	8–10
18. Seated Dumbbell Curl	4	6–8
19. Reverse Curl	3	6–8
20. Pulley Pushdown	4	8–10
21. Barbell Incline Triceps Extension	3–4	6–8
22. Barbell Wrist Curl	3	10–15
23. Barbell Reverse Wrist Curl	3	10–15
24. Standing Calf Machine	4	10–15
25. Seated Calf Machine	4	10–12

bodybuilding experience. At worst, you will merely discover that you don't enjoy doing so much training and that bodybuilding isn't for you. In that case, it's best to decide this early on, before you've invested several years of hard training in the sport!

ADVANCED ROUTINES

As you progress into the advanced level of training with weights—regardless of your ultimate goals in weight training—you will be doing so many sets for each body part that it becomes virtually impossible to do a full-body workout in a single training session. At that point, it's best to adopt a *split routine,* in which

Typically, half of the body is exercised on Mondays and Thursdays and the other half is trained on Tuesdays and Fridays.

There are numerous methods of splitting the body into halves. Three of the methods most commonly used are presented below.

A five-day split routine is another intensity progression up from a four-day split routine. In a five-day split, the body is divided into halves, as in a four-day split routine, and the halves are trained on alternate days, Monday through Friday. In a five-day split routine, then, one half of the body is trained three days one week, two the next week, three the third week, and so on. Designating the halves of the body "A" and "B," a chart is presented on page 125 showing how

Method A

Day 1 (*Pushing* muscles) | **Day 2** (*Pulling* muscles)

Chest — Thighs
Shoulders — Back
Triceps — Biceps
Forearms/Calves/Abs — Forearms/Calves/Abs

Method B

Day 1 (Torso muscles) | **Day 2** (Arms/Legs)

Chest — Thighs
Shoulders — Biceps
Back — Triceps
Forearms/Calves/Abs — Forearms/Calves/Abs

Method C

Day 1 (Emphasis on chest and shoulders as "weak" body parts) | **Day 2** (Remainder of body)

Chest — Thighs
Shoulders — Back
Calves/Abs — Upper Arms/Forearms
— Calves/Abs

you divide the body into halves or thirds and train only part of the body each day. This allows you to do shorter and more frequent workouts, but still gives each muscle group time to rest and recuperate. Since the muscle groups are done in rotation with a split routine, one muscle is resting on the day that another is trained, and 48–72 hours of rest is given to each muscle group before it is again trained.

The most basic split routine, one step up in intensity from three-days-per-week training, is a four-day split in which the body is divided into halves and each half is trained twice a week.

frequently the halves of the body can be trained during a four-week period.

There are two types of six-day split routines. In the first of these, which is the next intensity level progression up from five-day-per-week training, the body's major muscle groups are divided into three equal parts and each third of the body is trained twice a week (the calves, abdominals, and forearms can be exercised with weights four to six days per week on both six-day split routines).

Here is a typical example of how you can use a six-day split routine when training each major

	Monday	Tuesday	Wednesday
Week 1	A	B	A
Week 2	B	A	B
Week 3	A	B	A
Week 4	B	A	B

	Thursday	Friday
Week 1	B	A
Week 2	A	B
Week 3	B	A
Week 4	A	B

muscle group twice per week (Sunday is a rest day):

Monday-Thursday	Tuesday-Friday
Chest	Shoulders
Back	Upper Arms/Forearms
Calves/Abs	Calves/Abs

Wednesday-Saturday
Thighs
Forearms
Abs

On Wednesdays and Saturdays in the above routine, only one major muscle group is trained, which makes those seem like they would be easy days. Don't be fooled, however, because the thigh muscles are the largest in your body and require the greatest energy expenditure when properly trained. Therefore, leg training days can actually be tougher to survive than the chest/back and shoulder/arm training days.

In the second type of six-day split routine—usually followed only by competitive bodybuilders for the 4–6 weeks just prior to a contest when trying to peak out—the body is again split into halves and each half is trained on alternate days, resulting in three workouts per week for each major muscle group. Typically, half of the body is exercised on Mondays, Wednesdays, and Fridays, while the other half is trained on Tuesdays, Thursdays, and Saturdays. Sunday is a well-earned day of rest when on this type of six-day split routine.

Maximum Muscle Power

By using a four-day split routine to train your body for maximum strength, you can do much more intense workouts than during three-day-per-week training, and therefore you will make much faster progress. The following four-day split routine for strength training is typical of how you can use a split routine to help yourself to achieve any weight training goal, this time specifically a great strength increase:

Strength Training
(Four-Day Split Routine)

Monday-Thursday

Exercise	Sets	Reps
1. Incline Sit-Ups	2–3	20–30
2. Bench Press	6	6-5-4-3-2-1*
3. Incline Press	4	6-5-4-3*
4. Military Press	4	5-4-3-2*
5. Barbell Lying Triceps Extension	4	8-6-5-4*
6. Barbell Wrist Curl	3	10–15
7. Barbell Reverse Wrist Curl	3	10–15
8. Standing Calf Machine	5	8–12

Tuesday-Friday

Exercise	Sets	Reps
1. Incline Leg Raises	2–3	20–30
2. Hyperextension	1	15–20
3. Squat	6	6-5-4-3-2-1*
4. Deadlift	5	5-4-3-2-1*
5. Barbell Bent Rowing	5	8-6-5-4-4*
6. Barbell Curl	4	6-5-4-4*
7. Seated Calf Machine	5	8–12

*Pyramid weights and reps for these exercises.

WHAT'S NEXT?

In Chapter 5 we will present a large number of advanced training techniques, particularly in relation to competitive bodybuilding.

Boyer and Valerie Coe at the 1981 World Couples' Bodybuilding Championships.

Boyer Coe, Arnold Schwarzenegger, and Chris Dickerson posing down at the 1980 Mr. Olympia contest.

5
Advanced Training Techniques

In all probability, most of the readers of this book will be content to progress only to the training levels outlined in Chapters 2 through 4. A few dedicated men and women will, however, decide to become competitive bodybuilders. It is to this rare breed of individual that we dedicate the information in this chapter.

We will be covering a wide range of advanced training techniques and dietary practices in this chapter. We also will deal specifically with how we personally reach peak condition for bodybuilding competitions. By building upon the information contained in the preceding chapters, we feel you could actually use the advice and programs presented in this chapter to build a contest-winning physique, virtually without any additional coaching.

COMPETITIVE BODYBUILDING

Competitive bodybuilding contests are conducted on national and international levels for men, women, and couples (or *mixed pairs,* as couples are sometimes called). Within the United States hundreds of competitions are staged for amateur male and female bodybuilders, ranging from low-level, city championships to national championships that attract over 100 high-level competitors each year.

Scores of professional bodybuilding contests also are held for men, women, and couples on a worldwide basis each year. Many male and female professional bodybuilders are able to make a good living from the sport, and several currently earn more than $100,000 in a year. This money comes from a variety of sources, including prize money, guest posing fees, training seminar fees, endorsements, mail order businesses, and books like this.

It takes a rare breed of man or woman to be a competitive bodybuilder, particularly one who has developed to the point of winning various championships. High-level bodybuilders are incredibly disciplined individuals, capable of making virtually any sacrifice to reach the top level of bodybuilding. Competitive bodybuilders must almost *live* bodybuilding 24 hours a day—particularly before a contest is to be held—to be successful athletes.

What to Expect at a Competition

Every aspiring bodybuilder should attend several competitions—preferably ranging from the local to national levels—before venturing into competition themselves. This is necessary to familiarize yourself with how bodybuilding contests are conducted and judged. Without such an orientation period, you would undoubtedly embarrass yourself quite badly at your first competition.

Upcoming bodybuilding shows are advertised months in advance in weight training magazines. As soon as you discover one in your area, immediately purchase tickets for both the evening public presentation and the morning or afternoon prejudging sessions (in which most of the competition is actually judged). By buying tickets early, you will be assured of a good seat, centrally located in relation to the stage and as close to the stage as possible.

At each prejudging, seven certified judges are used. These judges are usually quite experienced, and they must take tests administered by the American Physique Committee (for men's amateur contests), American Federation of Women Bodybuilders (for amateur women's contests), or by the International Federation of Bodybuilders (IFBB) for pro and amateur men's and women's events.

The IFBB system of judging—which is also used in most amateur shows in America—provides for three major judging rounds, plus a final *posedown* round including the five top athletes—those with the highest cumulative scores—at the conclusion of Round III. In each round every judge awards from 1–20 points to every athlete. Then to prevent favoritism from influencing the outcome of a competition, the highest and lowest scores for each athlete are deleted and the remaining five scores are totaled for a *round score* of up to 100 points.

After three judging rounds an athlete could, therefore, accumulate 300 total points. Then in the posedown round, consisting of one to two minutes of concentrated and super-intense posing, each judge awards a first-place vote worth one additional point. So, an athlete can conceivably score a total of 307 points.

In toto, judges first look for balanced body proportions in a contestant, deleting points for underdeveloped calves, deltoids, and other body parts. Next, they look for muscularity, or the absence of fat over the muscles, then for total

In the 1981 World Cup, Boyer was the first . . .

muscle mass. Finally, they consider general appearance (grooming, tan, etc.) and posing ability. The three IFBB judging rounds are con-

. . . bodybuilder to score a perfect 307 points.

show their left sides, then their backs and right sides. In Round II each athlete must do strictly prescribed compulsory poses. These compulsories vary from men's to women's contests, as well as from year to year. Watch for and note what compulsory poses are being used just before you intend to compete and then practice these poses.

Round III is the *free posing* round in which every contestant poses individually for one to three minutes (depending on the level of competition) and to his or her own choice of recorded music. This round brings out the best creative abilities of each competitor as he or she attempts to display himself or herself with great personality and to maximum advantage. Take note of the types of poses each contestant does, as well as the artistic transitional moves between poses.

At most contests there will be guest posers, who are champion bodybuilders giving exhibitions of their posing ability and championship physiques. Watch these men and women very carefully, because they are masters of the art and sport of bodybuilding free posing.

Ultimately, a champion is chosen in each contest. Note how jubilant this man or woman is, because one day you will be onstage receiving your own first-place trophy. The thrill of victory in bodybuilding is so incredible to experience that it makes years of total dedication, Spartan dieting, hard training, and every personal sacrifice worthwhile!

Peaking

Every champion bodybuilder trains in cycles. For 3–9 months he or she will follow an off-season training and dietary philosophy aimed at attaining maximum muscle mass and bringing up weak body parts. And then for 6–12 weeks a competitive bodybuilder will follow a peaking philosophy aimed at reducing body fat levels to a minimum so every muscle group can be displayed in bold relief.

In the off-season, we feel that it's best to train most of the time on a four-day split routine, doing 10–15 total sets per muscle group. In general, concentrate more of your energies on your weak points than on your stronger muscle

structed to reveal all of these qualities in male and female bodybuilders quite clearly.

In Round I all of the athletes stand individually—and later in groups for comparisons—in a natural semirelaxed stance with the front of their bodies facing the judges. Then they turn to groups. Use primarily basic exercises (movements like squats, bench presses, and barbell bent rows that work large muscle groups in conjunction with smaller ones) and only a few isolation movements (exercises like leg extensions, dumbbell side laterals, and incline flyes that work one muscle—or even part of a muscle—in relative isolation from the rest of the body).

You should use maximum weights for reps primarily in the range of from 5–8. Rest 60–90 seconds between sets, and be sure to pyramid your weights and reps on heavy exercises. Pyramidding consists of progressively in-

creasing the weight while decreasing the reps with each succeeding set. Pyramidding is the easiest way to use heavy weights and progressively increase your training poundages at a fast rate.

Nutritionally, eat a balanced diet in the off-season, keeping at your caloric maintenance level, or perhaps slightly above it if you are trying to gradually increase your body weight. And if you crave some type of junk food in the off-season, go ahead and indulge yourself. Just be sure to hold such *junkouts* down to once or

twice a week, and never have more than one helping of any junk food.

Prior to competing, bodybuilders spend 6–12 weeks in a precontest cycle geared to melt away all body fat to produce a bodybuilder in totally peak shape on the day of a show. This peaking is accomplished by gradually intensifying training and tightening the diet, timing such changes to result in a peak on just the right day. As you can guess, contest peaking is an art.

You will probably need to peak out three or four times, taking detailed mental or written notes on factors influencing the timing of your peak, before you are able to time your peak very precisely. Valerie and I now peak instinctively according to how we look in the mirror at the beginning of each of the last six weeks before competing, and daily for the final week. If we look too fat at a checkpoint, we simply tighten the diet. And if we are losing body fat too quickly, we add to the number of calories we eat.

Precontest training should consist of a gradual and progressive intensification of each workout. From a four-day split routine, you might switch to a six-day split in which each major muscle group is trained twice a week and the calves, abdominals, and forearms are worked from 4–6 times a week. This automatically allows you to do more total sets for each body part, something you must do to help harden up your body for competition.

Obviously, you will need to experiment with contest countdown timing to determine what will work best for you, but for your first contest, switch to a six-day split about eight weeks before your competition. Stay on this split routine for four weeks, training each body part twice a week. Then for the final four weeks use a six-day split in which you train each muscle group three times a week. This will further harden your physique. A few professional bodybuilders will even follow a *double-split routine* in which they train twice a day for a few weeks before a competition. We will discuss double-split routines in detail later in this chapter.

During your contest countdown you must also gradually switch over from doing the large number of basic exercises of off-season training to using far more isolation movements. These isolation exercises don't build much muscle mass, but they are excellent for shaping and detailing individual muscle groups. Even just prior to a contest, however, you should still be doing one or two basic exercises per body part to maintain muscle mass while you are achieving contest cuts.

To be perfectly sure you understand the use of basic and isolation exercises in off-season and precontest training cycles, here are two sample chest-training routines:

Off-Season

Exercise	Sets	Reps
1. Incline Barbell Press*	4	6–8
2. Bench Press*	4	6–8
3. Parallel Bar Dips (weighted)*	3	8–10
4. Flyes	3	8–10

Precontest

Exercise	Sets	Reps
1. Bench Press*	4	6–10
2. Incline Flyes	3	10–12
3. Decline Flyes	3	10–12
4. Pec Deck Flyes	3	10–12
5. Incline Dumbbell Press*	3	8–10
6. Cable Crossovers	3	10–15

*Basic exercises.

While you are switching over from basic to isolation movements, you should also gradually increase the reps each set and decrease the rest intervals between sets. Some champion bodybuilders rest as little as 15–20 seconds between sets during peak precontest intensity. This fast training pace is called *quality training,* and such speedy training is essential for any bodybuilder who desires to reach peak muscular definition.

Several other intensity techniques, all discussed later in this chapter, also can be used when peaking out for a contest. All of them will contribute to increasing muscular definition. These techniques are peak contraction, continu-

ous tension, iso-tension contraction, supersets, trisets, giant sets, and pre-exhaustion.

A variety of precontest diets are used by competitive bodybuilders in an effort to reduce body fat to an absolute minimum. In fact, achieving peak contest muscularity is more than 75% a matter of diet. Unless you naturally have an exceedingly high rate of body metabolism, you will need to diet strictly for rather long periods of time to strip all of the fat from your body.

In the next major section of this chapter we will discuss advanced nutrition for bodybuilders in detail. For now, let us say that bodybuilders are about evenly split between using low-carbohydrate and low-fat (low-calorie) diets prior to a contest. We believe that you should give both types of diets a precontest trial before deciding which you will use for the remainder of your bodybuilding career.

The length of time you must remain on a

For better calf development, Boyer does a good deal of running with Legg shoes.

precontest diet will vary according to how much body fat you are initially carrying, how strictly you diet, and how good your body metabolism is. Try dieting for 4–6 weeks for your first competition, keeping very careful notes on how fast your body leans out in relation to the severity of your diet. Then when you compete a second time, you can adjust the length and severity of your diet according to the results of your first precontest dieting experience.

In addition to bodybuilding workouts and dieting, we have found that daily aerobic training is an essential part of the peaking process. Aerobic exercise, as you may recall from an earlier discussion, is a low-intensity physical activity that can be carried on for long periods of time within the body's capability of providing sufficient oxygen for the exercise. It actually burns more fat than an equivalent amount of anaerobic work (exercise of high enough intensity to build up an oxygen debt). Among top male and female bodybuilders, cycling and running are the most popular aerobic activities. Other good forms of aerobic exercise include swimming, jumping rope, mountain hiking, playing a racquet sport, and rowing.

We personally prefer stationary cycling for our precontest aerobic training. I spend one hour per day and Valerie two hours on our stationary bike when a competition or exhibition is coming up. I also do quite a bit of running with my Legg shoes.*

After peaking, we like to take a one-week layoff from training and gradually relax our diet. Be sure, however, that you don't eat too much or for too long after a contest, because adding an excessive amount of body fat will only make it more difficult to reach peak condition for your next show. After our layoff, we go back into our off-season training and dietary cycle and begin building up for another show.

Several years of cyclical training will give you a good degree of muscle mass and superb contest muscularity. If you have the native potential and are willing to work hard enough and diet

---

*Specially designed shoes that turn any run into a grueling calf workout; if you would like to try the Legg shoes, we can provide information on them; just write to me and Valerie Coe at P.O. Box 5877, Huntington Beach, California 92646.

strictly, cyclical training will ultimately turn you into a bodybuilding champion!

Contest Grooming and Appearance

In addition to having a super physique on-stage at a competition, there are several other appearance-related factors that will help you to win. General grooming is obviously one of these factors. Your hairstyle should be freshly maintained and in harmony with your general appearance. Beards and mustaches should be neatly trimmed, or a male contestant should have a fresh, clean shave.

A woman bodybuilder is required to wear her hair either short or pinned up so the judges can clearly see the shoulder and upper back muscles. Some women adorn their hair with a flower. Experiment with various flowers and hairstyles before competing, and pick the combination most flattering for you. *Do not,* however, *wear jewelry onstage* (this applies to men, too), because it can distract a judge's attention from your physique.

Because bodybuilding contest lighting—particularly for the individual free-posing round of judging—is quite harsh, a woman may need to apply makeup more boldly than she normally would. If you've seen a dancer or stage actor/actress after a performance, you will note that their makeup is far more heavy and dark than normal. Again, experiment with varying degrees of makeup from contest to contest, until you discover a formula that works well for you.

Women shave their bodies automatically in everyday life, but some men balk at the idea of shaving down for a bodybuilding contest. This is essential, however, because a thick mat of body hair will obscure your hard-earned muscularity. It's best to shave down several weeks before a contest, then you can use an electric razor every two or three days to maintain the shave. Shaving early will allow you to obtain a more even tan, and it gives any knicks and cuts you might give yourself plenty of time to heal. Your initial body shave should be done with a double-edged razor on dry skin. You'll probably have to change the blade a couple of times, but this dry-shaving method—when used carefully—will give you a clean body shave with few knicks or cuts.

Some bodybuilders use *depilatories* (chemical hair removers) instead of shaving. This method of hair removal is fine as long as you are not allergic to the chemicals in the cream. Many men and women develop skin rashes from them. Try it on a small area of your body *a month or more* before your competition to see if you have an allergy.

Choice of posing attire is important, because the wrong posing suit can detract from your physique or hide part of your muscular development. Better men's and women's clothing shops have a variety of swim wear that will be appropriate for posing. A majority of the female champions seem to wear Kamali swimsuits. Male posing suits can also be ordered through bodybuilding magazines.

There are several key factors to consider when choosing posing attire. It should be of a solid color, since patterns are as distracting as jewelry. The color should harmonize with your skin, eye, and hair coloring. And the suit should be cut briefly enough that it doesn't cover any of your upper thigh or lower abdominal muscularity.

Another appearance factor to be considered is a tan. Black men and women—or others with naturally dark skin—needn't worry about tanning, but a good tan will make fair-skinned persons like ourselves look much harder and more healthy onstage. Pure white skin can actually make a bodybuilder appear soft, particularly under a posing light.

A natural tan is best. Start lying out in the sun each day at least six weeks before your competition. Begin with only about 10 minutes of sun for each side of your body, then gradually build up your sunbathing time until you can take two to three hours of sun without burning.

When sunbathing, protect your skin from drying out by using a tanning oil. Most oils have a sunscreening agent in them, so if you're particularly fair and susceptible to sunburn, use an oil with a high sunscreening factor. We know from repeated experience that sunbathing can be monotonous and boring, but a rich, deep-brown tan at contest time is well worth the effort you have to expend to acquire it.

Artificial salon tans can be good, particularly for winter contests. They are rather expensive to acquire, however, and the harm that they can cause to human skin has been widely debated.

As a last resort, you can give yourself an artificial chemical tan. These bronzing creams and instant-tan agents either stain the skin or act as a sort of makeup. Most of them will also tan your clothing and other fabrics (bed sheets, beach blankets, etc.), and they turn areas where the skin is thickest (knees, elbows, hands, etc.) far more dark than other parts of the body. Most chemical tanning preparations also result in a yellow or orange—rather than brown—tan.

If you use a chemical tanning preparation, be sure to wear rubber gloves when applying it, or have someone else wear the gloves to apply it. Put on two or three coats of the chemical, being sure to put less of it on your hands, knees, ankles, and elbows. Be sure to apply some to your face and feet, too. We once saw a top-level male bodybuilder who had a magnificent (although yellowish) tan over all of his body except his face, which was lily white. He looked almost as if some giant person had held him by the head and dipped him up to his neck in a vat of nicotine!

The final detail of contest appearance that you should master is the use of body oil. Even a Mr. Olympia competitor would look as flat as a board if he didn't use oil for his competitions and posing exhibitions. Applied evenly and to the proper degree, this oil will highlight every nuance of muscular detail that you have developed through your diet and training. Oil that is applied too heavily or unevenly will, however, make you look like a clown. Vegetable oils are far better than mineral- or petroleum-based oils, because they readily soak into the skin. This gives your skin a healthy, glowing appearance, which ideally highlights your muscularity. Other oils lie on the skin, making it look too shiny and throwing off glaring highlights under the posing light. Try using almond, avocado, sesame, or some other vegetable oil. You'll end up looking much better under contest lighting.

As with virtually every other bodybuilding factor, you will need to experiment with your

from contest to contest. If you can take the
person with you to every contest, it's best
him or her oil you. It's much easier for
else to apply oil evenly to your body,
y to your back, than it is for you to
urself. And once your oiler masters
look great onstage at every com-

r we discussed the three
have to do at a compe-
out how you should
ses. It is necessary
cause posing can
If Valerie and I
e seen a very
ose clumsily
r man or
ould be
idente

gth mirror—
clearly see your
ch to practice your
y mirror two feet wide
will cost less than $40 at a
g in glass and mirrors. A posing

Boyer, considered one of the best posers in bodybuilding,
performs a double-biceps lunge at the 1980 Mr. Olympia
contest.

light (usually a flood light) will also be quite
helpful when practicing. Set it so the light falls
on your body from above at approximately a
45-degree angle. This will give you an accurate
knowledge of the highlights and shadows the
judges will see on your body when you are
posing onstage.

Then begin to look closely at the photos of
champion bodybuilders published each month
in bodybuilding magazines. Pick a few of their
poses, then try to duplicate them in front of
your mirror. Because of your unique physical
structure, you may look better in some poses
than in others. Keep the good poses for your
routine and discard the rest until later, when
your development has improved enough to allow you to do them a little better.

Every pose you see in magazines and onstage
at a contest must be *adapted* to your physique.
Cut out ten photographs of champion male or
female bodybuilders doing the same pose and
place them side by side. You should immediately
notice that each champion does the pose a little
differently from the rest. A slight shift in hand
or foot position, a twist of the waist or hips,
movement of the arms slightly more forward or
backward, or any number of other minor
changes can drastically improve the way you
look in a particular pose.

The only way you can come up with an
adaptation of any pose that perfectly suits your
physique is to pose every day in front of your
mirror for at least 30 minutes. Close to a competition, Val and I practice posing for up to two
hours a day. This practice has paid off, because
we are often complimented on the excellence of
our individual and dual posing routines.

When you first begin to practice posing,
spend the bulk of your time mastering the
Round I semirelaxed stances and the Round II
compulsory poses. Most champion bodybuilders
base their Round III free-posing routines on the
compulsory poses, so it's absolutely essential to
master these stances.

Once you have developed a repertoire of
individual poses, you will need to string them
together into a free-posing routine. We can tell
you how to do this, but first we must caution
you to never over-pose. Much too often novice
bodybuilders jump onstage and do routines
consisting of 30 poses, 6–8 of which do them

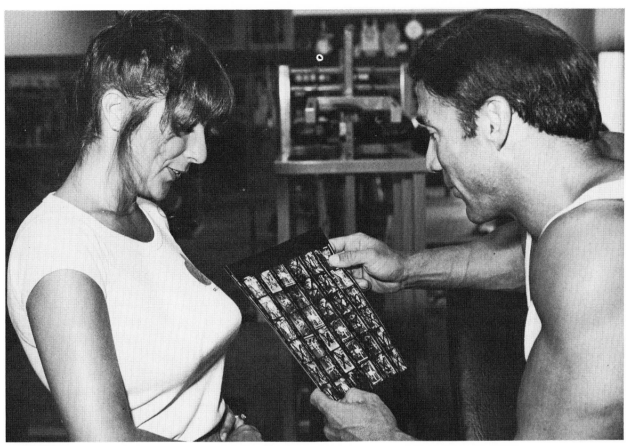

Part of pro bodybuilding is posing for thousands of photos each year.

some good and the rest of which make them look worse than they really are.

In your first contest, it is far better to do from 8-10 good poses that display all four sides of your body than to do from 20-30 mediocre poses. As your physique and posing ability improve, you can gradually add new poses to your routine. The true superstars of bodybuilding are able to do up to 30-40 superb poses, but these men and women have put in many years of hard training and consistent posing practice to master that many poses. But even these champions will *never* do a pose that fails to present their physiques to best advantage.

The factor that can make or break a free-posing routine is the transitional movement between each pose. These transitions should be both smooth and artistic. Ultimately, you will develop unique transitions, but initially you should copy the transitional movements of the better posers you see at various contests. And if you find it difficult to remember these transitions, 8mm films of champion bodybuilders doing their routines are available through ads in

bodybuilding magazines.

A background of dance instruction—particularly ballet and jazz dance—can be invaluable when evolving innovative transitions between poses. If you don't have this background, you can still benefit from dance techniques. Most dance studios offer private lessons for about $20 each, and dance teachers welcome the challenge of working with a bodybuilder who's trying to develop an innovative posing routine. Several high-level bodybuilders in recent years have had dance instructors choreograph their posing routines.

In most contests, you will be allowed to pose to your choice of music, which you will provide on a cassette. It's a good idea to always bring a spare cassette of your music, because many sound systems have eaten a bodybuilder's tape.

Your choice of music should fit your personality, and the song should last about 90 seconds for amateur contestants and two to three minutes for pro bodybuilders. Instrumental music is usually chosen over vocal music, but either type of music can be used. The key to music choice is that it fit your personality, and you can choreograph your posing to exactly match the tempo of your music.

Ultimately, your free-posing routine is an extension of your personality. It should be as innovative and exciting to watch as possible, and it can win or lose a competition for you. So, don't be afraid to practice your posing long and hard.

ADVANCED NUTRITION

Most champion bodybuilders agree that a proper approach to nutrition is at least 75% of the battle, particularly in terms of achieving contest definition. Entire books have been written on the subject, and several articles on advanced nutrition are carried in each issue of *Muscle & Fitness* magazine. We will give you a good beginning on the subject of advanced nutrition, but you should refine it with further study.

One of the biggest secrets in bodybuilding is the realization that no single dietary or training technique will work for every bodybuilder. My specific diet doesn't work identically for Valerie, or for other male bodybuilders like Mike Mentzer or Roy Callender. And Val's diet doesn't work for champion bodybuilders like Laura Combes or Rachel McLish.

Therefore, we will give you general, advanced nutritional guidelines in this chapter, and then it becomes your responsibility to determine the exact dietary philosophy that works best for you. As in developing a training philosophy, this involves trying every possible food element in your diet for a few weeks at a time to decide if, and how well, it works for you.

During a two- or three-week trial with a food element, you can monitor your body's biofeedback to determine what effect that food or supplement has had on your body. As an example, if you ate a pint of pistachio ice cream every day for three weeks, a certain piece of biofeedback data (the fact that you're growing incredibly fat) will tell you that food's effect on your body.

Try to decide if a new food element gives you

A toast to nutrition, one of the keys to vibrant health.

greater workout energy. Does it allow you to sleep better and recuperate more completely? Does it make your skin more healthy looking? Does it help to define you before a show, or does it prevent you from achieving maximum muscular definition? How does it affect your range of emotions? By monitoring all of the biofeedback that your body eventually provides you, you can develop an instinct for how a training or dietary factor is working in your body. Instinctive training ability—for both training and diet—is one of the most valuable skills any bodybuilder can develop.

Protein Requirements

There is an incredible diversity of opinion on just how much and what types of protein are needed each day by bodybuilders. For instance, Bill Pearl (a Mr. America and four-time Mr. Universe winner) feels that even a bodybuilder weighing over 200 pounds can make gains in muscle mass on as little as 50 grams of protein each day. And he believes that this protein can come primarily from milk products and vegetable sources. On the other side of the coin, Dave Johns (a former Mr. America and Mr. USA winner) eats up to 50 *eggs* a day and feels he needs an average of 350–400 grams of protein per day to make gains from his training.

Our personal feelings on protein requirements are moderate. Weighing a little over 200 pounds for competition, I consume 150–200 grams of protein a day. Valerie, 85 pounds lighter, eats 80–100 grams of protein each day.

There is absolutely no doubt that protein is a vital food element for every bodybuilder. Protein forms the building blocks for all of the body's skeletal muscles (over 600 of them), as well as for every major organ (e.g., the heart, lungs, kidneys, skin, eyes, stomach, etc.). The Food and Drug Administration (FDA) has set an Adult Minimum Daily Requirement (AMDR) for protein consumption at one gram per kilogram (2.2 pounds) of body weight. In other words, the FDA's AMDR is a little less than a half gram of protein per pound of body weight. The FDA also believes that much of this protein AMDR can be made up from vegetable protein sources.

We personally feel that active bodybuilders require almost twice as much protein as what the FDA recommends, and we believe that this protein should come primarily from animal sources, which yield a higher quality of protein than do vegetable sources. We recommend that you eat three-quarters to one gram of protein per pound of body weight. Any diet amounting to 300–400 grams of protein a day is a waste of money, as well as a potential strain on the kidneys. It also can be a potential source of accumulated body fat because *all* calories in excess of daily energy requirements will be stored as body fat, whether they come from fats, carbohydrates, or proteins.

You should always consider the quality of the protein that you eat. Nutritionists talk about the Protein Efficiency Ratio (PER) of foods, which is based on each food's amino acid content and assimilability by the body. Amino acids are the building blocks of protein itself. There are 22 amino acids, 14 of which the human body can produce within its own digestive system. The other eight—called *essential amino acids*—can't be manufactured in the body and must be contained in the food you eat.

If even one essential amino acid is missing from the food you eat, your body won't be able to use the protein that you have consumed. For body assimilation of protein, you must consume either a food containing all eight essential amino acids or a combination of foods that supply a few of these essential amino acids, which, when totaled, have all eight essential amino acids.

This is where the PER of foods comes into play in planning the protein content of your diet. It so happens that all proteins from animal sources are complete (contain all of the essential amino acids in high concentrations). Egg albumen (egg white) has the highest PER, followed fairly closely by milk products and then by animal flesh (meat, fish, poultry, etc.).

Of all vegetable proteins, only soya beans have complete protein, although this food's content of one of the essential amino acids is quite low. All other vegetable proteins (nuts, seeds, grains, beans, corn, etc.) contain incomplete proteins. It is possible to improve the completeness and the usefulness of vegetable proteins by combining them with either complete animal proteins or with other vegetable protein sources with complementary amino acid makeups. Here are three such combinations that are used, particularly in underdeveloped countries: (1) Grains + milk products, (2) Grains + legumes (peas, beans, etc.), and (3) Seeds + legumes.

We encourage bodybuilders to avoid—or at least curtail their consumption of—red meats, such as beef and pork. These red meats are extremely fatty, and therefore quite high in calories. They also contain considerable uric acid, which harms the body's joints. A bodybuilder's best sources of protein are fish, poultry (with the fatty skin removed before baking or broiling), eggs, and commercial protein supplements.

Milk presents problems to most bodybuilders, because 90%–95% of all men and women are at least mildly allergic to the lactose (milk sugar) in it. This can cause both stomach and skin bloating, because most adults have insufficient production of lactase, the enzyme that digests lactose. Milk products without lactose (cheese, protein powders, etc.) will present no allergy problems.

Protein supplements are useful to bodybuilders if they are used correctly and not to excess. When you are eating five to six (or more) meals per day in an attempt to gain muscular body weight, a protein drink is valuable between regular meals. Or if you're so rushed that you would ordinarily not have time to prepare a meal, a protein drink can be whipped up and consumed in as little as three or four minutes. And it will give you nearly as much nutritional value as the meal you would have missed.

Protein (and all other) supplements should always be used as *supplements,* however, not as substitutes for ordinary, nutritional foods. The tendency of some young and enthusiastic bodybuilders is to get so carried away using food supplements that they virtually exist on supplements alone. Some spend over $1000 per month on food supplements, which is very foolish.

To properly mix a protein drink, you will need a blender, which is often called "the bodybuilder's best friend." If you don't already have one, buy a good quality blender with variable speed controls. You'll use your blender a lot, so it's better to spend more money on one now than to economize and have the cheaper blender break down after only a few months of use.

Since milk and eggs have the highest PERs, we feel that a milk-and-egg protein powder of at least 90% protein content is best for use in protein drinks. If this protein is sweetened by *anything,* it should be fructose (fruit sugar). Using your protein powder, here is a good recipe for protein drinks:

1. Eight to ten ounces of raw milk (unpasteurized) or fruit juice (apple juice is best)
2. One to two tablespoons of protein powder
3. Flavoring (optional)

Bodybuilders use numerous flavorings, including chocolate syrup, maple extract, artificial vanilla syrup, and various flavors of ice cream. We feel that fresh natural fruit makes the best tasting and most nutritious flavorings for protein drinks. Soft fruits like bananas, strawberries, and peaches are the best fruits for blender use as flavorings in protein drinks.

Carbohydrates and Fats

Carbohydrates and fats are the body's main sources of energy, with carbohydrates the body's preferred energy source. One gram of carbohydrate yields four calories when metabolized for energy in the human body. One gram of fat yields nine calories.

Carbohydrates are easily metabolized by the body and produce energy very quickly. As such, carbohydrates are the best source of fuel for workout energy. I consume about 150 grams of carbohydrates each day when dieting for contests and even greater quantities of carbohydrates in the off-season. Valerie eats 80–90 grams of carbohydrate during her competition-dieting cycle.

There are two major categories of carbohydrates—*simple* (or refined, e.g., white flour, white sugar, and alcohol) and *complex* (or natural, e.g., fresh fruits, vegetables, whole grains, and salads). Simple carbohydrates give the body nothing but calories, because most of the vitamins and minerals have been removed from them when the foods have been processed. We avoid simple carbohydrates like the plague year-round.

Fresh fruit, vegetables, and salads are the best complex carbohydrates for precontest dieting. As with milk, 90%–95% of men and women are at least mildly allergic to grains, and grain allergies will cause retention of excess water in the body. Body water can actually make a well-defined physique look smooth and bloated.

High-roughage fruits and vegetables are vital in the diet. These include pears, celery, and lettuce. Pure grain bran is also a good source of roughage (a cellulose-type of carbohydrate that can't be digested in the human stomach and therefore passes through the body, adding to stool bulk). Celery and most salad greens actually require more energy to digest than they produce and are thus *negative calorie* foods.

A certain amount of fats is necessary for healthy skin and proper nerve function, but we both severely limit fat intake when dieting for contests. It is impossible to completely eliminate fats from the diet—and, indeed, it would be unhealthy to do so—but we go as close to zero fat intake as possible. This is done, of course, because fats have more than twice as many calories per gram as protein and carbohydrates.

Low-Fat Dieting

As we mentioned earlier, eliminating beef and pork from the diet will significantly reduce the diet's fat content. Other high-fat foods include full-fat milk products (including butter and cheese), cooking and salad oils, egg yolk, nuts, seeds, grains, corn, avocados, bananas, shortening, and cream substitutes for coffee. Consumption of all of these foods should be gradually cut back, or completely eliminated, when on a low-fat diet.

Overall, low-fat dieting is the best way to eliminate the body's fat stores while maintaining maximum muscle mass. Valerie and I follow the low-fat diet prior to competition. Here's a typical day's menu when on a low-fat diet (the amounts of each food actually eaten vary according to sex, relative body mass, and severity of the diet):

Meal One—broiled fish, fruit, supplements, and water

Snack—one piece of fruit

Meal Two—tuna salad made with water-packed tuna, fruit, supplements, and iced tea (artifi-

cially sweetened, or with lemon)

Snack—piece of fruit or a dry, baked potato

Meal Three—broiled chicken breast, green salad, supplements, and coffee or iced tea

You can adapt the above sample diet to your own requirements and situation. Simply experiment with various amounts and types of low-fat foods and use your instinct and body appearance to determine what exact diet you should follow.

The following are 10 dietary hints that we can suggest for use when following a low-fat diet:

1. If choosing between pork and beef, eat beef because it is lower in calories. Similarly, chicken and turkey have less fat than beef (poultry white meat has less fat content than the dark meat, too), and fish is even lower in fat content than poultry. Remove the fatty skin of all poultry before cooking it.

2. Never fry foods, because they soak up the cooking oil, significantly raising the caloric content of the food. Always bake or broil poultry and fish. Charcoal broiling adds a particularly nice flavor to all foods.

3. Don't use butter or any full-fat milk products. If you must use milk products, be sure that they are made from non-fat milk (e.g., mozzarella cheese). Overall, you should avoid all milk products, particularly for the last two weeks before competing. Milk tends to hold excess water in the body.

4. Never use oils or commercial dressings on salads. To a salad base, add parsley and other herbs, then vinegar and/or lemon juice. This will make any salad quite palatable, and many bodybuilders feel that vinegar helps to metabolize body fat.

5. Eat baked potatoes plain, without butter, margarine, or sour cream (all of which are high in fat). Dry baked potatoes actually taste quite good once you get used to them. Adding butter or sour cream can double the caloric content of a potato.

6. Use as many herbs and spices as possible in your cooking, because each will impart a distinct taste to ordinary fish or chicken. Additionally, herbs and spices have almost negligible caloric content.

7. If you must eat bread, buy whole-grain, flourless bread in a health food store and eat it plain or toasted. Be sure the bread has been baked without the addition of butter or shortening. When you do eat bread, never put butter, peanut butter, jelly, jam, honey, or anything else on it. These bread spreads can double or triple the caloric content of a slice of bread. Avoid all grain products when on a precontest diet, particularly for the last two weeks before a show. As we have mentioned, grains tend to bloat the body with excess water, which would be disastrous at contest time.

8. Don't boil vegetables, because that leaches out many of the vitamins and minerals these vegetables contain. Of course you should never use butter or oil on cooked vegetables. Instead of boiling them, either lightly steam your vegetables or eat them raw.

9. Avoid using sodium (table salt, artificial sweeteners) in your diet, and avoid high-sodium foods like celery. One gram of sodium will retain 50 grams of water in your body for two to three days. Avoid all sugar substitutes, diet sodas, and table salt, particularly for the last two weeks prior to competing.

10. Every bodybuilder gets cravings when on a precontest diet, particularly for sugar and fats. Don't fall prey to such cravings, however, because weakening just once will lead to blowing your diet time after time. There are numerous naturally sweet fruits which will quickly assuage any cravings you might have for sweets. Try watermelon, strawberries, or peaches. A serving of one or two of these fruits will get your mind off ice cream and back on your competition diet quite quickly.

Within the framework for precontest dieting that we've provided here, there are numerous ways you can fine tune the diet. Any book with food calorie tables will give you plenty of ideas for lowering caloric content in a diet, even over and above limiting fats. As an example, fruits and vegetables like strawberries, melons, seed sprouts, mushrooms, spinach, and tomatoes are much lower in caloric content than bananas, avocados, apricots, dates, and sweet potatoes.

Low-Carbohydrate Dieting

Until recent years, the standard precontest diet for bodybuilding was the low-carbohydrate diet in which carbohydrates were severely restricted in the daily diet or eliminated completely. Large numbers of bodybuilders have gotten cut up on this diet, but only with great strain on their minds and bodies, and not without a considerable loss of muscle mass.

The theory behind low-carb dieting is that fats in food that's eaten can't be used for energy or stored in the body in the absence of carbohydrates, thereby forcing the body to metabolize its own stored fat for energy. So, such foods as beef, eggs, and water are eaten for several weeks, and ultimately a bodybuilder loses body fat. Initially, he or she loses weight very rapidly, but later this rate of weight loss greatly decelerates. And everyone we've ever known who was on a low-carbohydrate diet had very little energy, was as touchy as one big raw nerve, and always felt generally miserable.

Weight is lost quickly the first week, because carbohydrates hold water in the body at a rate of four grams of water for each gram of carbohydrate. Thus, with carbohydrate deprivation, the body is unable to retain its accustomed supply of water and flushes it out rather rapidly. This causes the quick initial weight loss.

Carbohydrate deprivation is very hard on the body, however, because carbohydrates are the body's preferred source of energy. Without them it's impossible to put in a decently intense bodybuilding workout. Because you can't train hard—and due to the fact that muscle tissue is actually used up to provide energy when on a low-carb diet—muscle mass can be lost very quickly. Maximum muscle mass can best be retained on a low-calorie diet with moderate carbohydrate content.

Carbohydrate deprivation also has a very negative effect on the brain, which requires certain blood sugar levels for normal function. When carbohydrates don't provide this sugar to the brain, the mind can be dulled and becomes prone to wild swings in mood. Depression is common among low-carbohydrate dieters. When the blood sugar reaches critically low levels, binge eating becomes virtually a means of survival.

Overall, low-carbohydrate dieting is unhealthy for any human being and ineffective for bodybuilders. We strongly recommend that you avoid it. Use a low-fat diet instead. You'll be able to reach peak muscularity on it while retaining maximum muscle size. And onstage at a bodybuilding contest, that's an unbeatable combination.

Vitamins and Minerals

Champion bodybuilders take a wide variety of vitamins, minerals, and other food supplements. This is particularly true in the weeks leading up to a competition, when the diet must be severely limited to bring out maximum muscularity. Because less nutrients can be derived from actual food, they must be added to the diet via food supplements.

Most top bodybuilders take two or three times the amount of vitamins and minerals prior to competition that they consume in the off-season. This is particularly true of those bodybuilders who still follow the old-fashioned, low-carbohydrate diet, because they can't eat any fresh fruits or vegetables. Therefore, they lose out on many vitamins, minerals, and enzymes contained in those foods. The loss of digestive enzymes is particularly crucial, so it's essential for low-carb dieters to supplement their diet with digestive enzymes.

In the off-season we feel that any bodybuilder can easily avoid dietary deficiencies by consuming one or two multipacks of vitamins, minerals, and trace elements daily. You might also feel the need for extra vitamin C (between 2000 and 5000 milligrams a day), vitamin B complex, and chelated multiple minerals.

Overall, you must use your instinct to arrive at individualized supplementation schedules. This involves trying one new supplement at a time for a week or two in your diet, then deciding if it adds to your training energy and/or muscle mass gains.

The degree to which you go into food supplementation obviously will be limited by your pocketbook, because they *are* expensive. So you can know which individual supplements to try in your diet, here is a list of those most commonly used by champion bodybuilders and the effects each supplement might have on your body:

Multipacks—As we've said, this is basic nutritional insurance against dietary deficiencies. If you don't use multipacks, at least use two or three multiple vitamin-mineral tablets or capsules each meal. As with all such supplements, consume them during your meal for best absorption.

Dessicated Liver—Liver is an amazing source of energy, as proven by German scientists many years ago. Briefly, they fed three groups of lab rats different diets—one the regular lab diet, the second group the regular diet plus synthetic vitamins, and the third group the regular diet plus dessicated liver. Then they put the rats in drums of water from which they could not escape. To survive, the rats had to keep swimming; it was an emphatic test of endurance. The group of rats on dessicated liver swam many times longer before drowning than either of the other two groups. Some liver-eating rats were still swimming vigorously after two hours, when the test was concluded! Dessicated liver is approximately 70% high-quality protein and 30% carbohydrate, and a rich source of natural B-complex vitamins and iron.

Kelp—Dried sea kelp tablets are excellent sources of minerals and trace elements. They are particularly high in iodine content. Some nutritionists believe that iodine speeds up the body's metabolism, while others feel it actually slows down the body's basal metabolic rate (BMR). Experiment with kelp yourself and see if it helps you to reach peak muscular definition.

Vitamin B Complex—These vitamins are vital to all bodybuilders. They form enzymes within the body, and stimulate a healthy appetite. Since B vitamins are water-soluble, they must be taken frequently throughout the day or in timed-release form.

Potassium and Magnesium—These two minerals are called *electrolytes* and are essential for electrical energy conduction in the body, particularly in the heart. If your workouts have been dragging, try taking potassium and magnesium tablets before going to the gym. Usually they will increase your training energy levels.

Manganese—This mineral is essential for joint and connective tissue health and resilience to injury. If you develop sore joints, supplementation with chelated manganese might solve the problem.

Vitamin C—For recuperation from workouts and general body detoxification from air and water pollution, vitamin C is essential. It can be taken in large dosages, but since it's water-soluble you must take it frequently during the day or in timed-release form. Vitamin C should always be taken in a form that includes the bioflavonoids (vitamin K), because in nature vitamin C and vitamin K always occur together.

Choline and Inositol—These two B-complex vitamins aid in fat metabolism, and many bodybuilders take them in high amounts prior to contests as an aid to getting completely cut up.

Vitamins A and D—Usually derived from fish liver oils, these vitamins promote healthy skin and hair, requisites to success in bodybuilding competition. They are also essential to eye health. These are fat-soluble vitamins that will be stored in the body, however, so you probably won't need to take mass quantities except before a competition. If you sunbathe a lot, you won't even need to take vitamin D, because it's produced in the skin when you are exposed to the sun's rays.

Vitamins B^{12} and B^{15}—Many bodybuilders feel that these two B-complex vitamins help to promote greater workout energy and endurance. Recently, B^{15}, in particular, has enjoyed great popularity.

Vitamin E—Another oil-soluble vitamin that supposedly increases workout endurance is vitamin E. Vitamin E (particularly the *d-alpha tocopherol* component) is essential for optimum heart and vascular health and function. Vitamin E also is essential for healthy sexual function, particularly in men.

Iron—This mineral is essential for proper oxygen transfer and transport in the bloodstream, so it also increases training energy. (Some nutritionists believe that iron and vitamin E taken at the same time cancel out each other's effects. Take them at widely separated times of the day, just in case they're right.) Iron is particularly important to menstruating women, since it is eliminated during menstruation. Generally speaking, women are usually deficient in iron levels in their bodies.

Calcium—This mineral is essential for strong and healthy teeth and bones. During precontest dieting, it can have a calming effect on the body. Animal proteins are very high in phosphorous, which builds up during a precontest diet and causes jitters. Calcium counteracts the effects of phosphorous and has a calming effect on the nerves.

Tryptophane—One of the eight essential amino acids, *tryptophane* is a natural tranquilizer. Many bodybuilders who experience difficulty sleeping, particularly when they are nervous just before competition, use three to five tryptophane tablets to induce sleep.

Ribonucleic Acid (RNA)—RNA is an ingredient essential to muscle hypertrophy. Many bodybuilders are now supplementing their diets with RNA tablets and experiencing good results from using this supplement.

Buying Supplements Inexpensively

Food supplements bought for full-price at a health food store or gym can be quite expensive. But there's a way to buy supplements for a 40%–60% discount. Simply organize a group of friends and pool your money to buy supplements at wholesale rates in case lots from wholesale jobbers. Many bodybuilders have done this over the years, saving themselves thousands of dollars in the process.

Hair Analysis

There is a test for mineral uptake within the human body that identifies deficiencies in dietary minerals. This test involves a spectrographic analysis of a hair sample (usually of pubic hair, which isn't exposed to air pollutants). This hair analysis test costs between $30 and $100, depending on where you have it done. Almost any medical lab can make this hair analysis for you. It's a valuable test, because when deficiencies are identified, you can take extra supplements of the deficient mineral, which often results in immediately accelerated gains in strength and muscle mass. More often than not, nutritional deficiencies are from insufficient mineral (not vitamin) intake. If this test interests you, ask your family physician about having one done.

INSTINCTIVE TRAINING

As mentioned earlier in this book, training instinct (as well as dietary instinct) is merely an ability to recognize and interpret the biofeedback signals your body is constantly giving you. What does pain in a muscle or joint mean to you? Is it an injury pain, or merely the burn of fatigue toxins building up within a working muscle? Pain is just one example of the numerous types of biofeedback your body gives you and how this biofeedback is interpreted by an intelligent bodybuilder.

The three best indicators of whether or not an exercise routine is working for you are *muscle pump,* muscle soreness, and observable muscle growth.

All bodybuilders are constantly seeking a good pump. A good muscle pump (a tight, blood-congested feeling in a muscle) is a sure indication that you have given a muscle group a good workout. This pump is caused by an influx of blood into a trained muscle to remove waste products and replace used-up fuel supplies (*glycogen*) in the muscles.

Muscle soreness after a workout—as long as it hasn't been caused by an injury—is another sure indication of muscle growth from a workout. And you can even observe small changes in the density (hardness), contour, and size of a muscle group from week to week.

By observing changes in your body and relating your body's biofeedback data to various exercise and nutritional stimuli for a year or two, you can develop an instinctive *feel* for how a new stimulus affects your body. Then you will have developed instinctive training ability, which is very valuable to any competitive bodybuilder. Instinctive training ability allows you to determine the worth of a new training or nutritional stimulus within a workout or two, saving you the weeks of experimentation that beginning and intermediate bodybuilders must invest in each new technique.

BODYBUILDING POTENTIAL

Every man and woman has a unique, inherent potential for competitive bodybuilding. As in any other sport, your physical potential can make or break you as a bodybuilder. Your bodybuilding potential will determine whether or not you can be an outstanding, competitive bodybuilder, how quickly you can achieve a quality physique, and the ultimate degree to which you can develop your body.

It will be difficult for you to evaluate your skeletal structure, a major factor in bodybuilding potential, but any experienced bodybuilder can do it for you with only a glance. Man or woman, it's best if you have a medium-sized bone structure with small joints. This will allow you to build the most esthetic type of physique. With such a bone structure, you can develop a body like a thoroughbred race horse, rather than a Shetland pony or a Percheron.

In an untrained state, a male bodybuilder's shoulders should be as wide as his hips, or wider. A woman's shoulders should be similarly broad, but it's a very rare occurrence to see a woman with the relative skeletal shoulder width of a man. Limb length should be moderate in relation to the torso's proportion. It would look quite odd for a male or female bodybuilder to have the relative arm length of an orangutan.

You will achieve the best type of physique if your muscles have length, plus the ability to achieve peaks. Some bodybuilders have muscle insertions that make the muscle masses very short, e.g., the typical high calf that many black bodybuilders have. With such short muscles, it becomes difficult to develop a complete-looking physique.

Having long muscles without the ability to develop peaks also prevents a bodybuilder from achieving maximum impressiveness. Sergio Oliva often has been referred to as a bodybuilder with great genetic gifts for the sport. Still, his biceps—while marvelously full in their development—never had peaks, giving him one shortcoming. Some bodybuilders even have arms that peak on one side and are flat on the other. Arnold Schwarzenegger is a good example of a bodybuilder with such odd arm development.

The ability to gain muscle mass fairly quickly is another genetically determined trait. Even though your diet and training influences the rate at which you make muscle gains, the ultimate speed at which you put on muscle mass is genetically determined. And some bodybuilders are simply unable to build quality muscle tissue quickly enough to keep them interested in bodybuilding training over the long haul.

Any man who gains 10–15 pounds of muscle (women's figures should be about 50% of men's) in his first year of training can be characterized as a fairly fast gainer, and thus one with potential as a bodybuilder. Over the many years that they train, most champion male bodybuilders have gained five to six pounds of muscle mass per year. Anything less than this rate of gain can ultimately doom you to failure as a bodybuilder. I gained approximately 10 pounds of muscle in my first year of training, while Val lost five pounds and greatly increased her strength and muscle tone.

The ability to gain muscle mass evenly in every body part is also important. Numerous specialization techniques can be used to bring a lagging body part up to the level of the rest of your body, *if* that body part can be improved. Unfortunately, some bodybuilders are born with a muscle group that will never equal the development of the rest of their body.

In addition to physical factors, modern bodybuilders must possess a high degree of mental ability if they hope to reach the top in their sport. The sport now relies so heavily on scientific disciplines that a successful bodybuilder must be able to understand and use the techniques of such complicated scientific subjects as biomechanics, kinesiology, anatomy, exercise physiology, psychology, and biochemistry. Clearly, a man or woman of less than average intelligence will never be able to use scientific research to advantage in the gym, and thus will not reach his or her true physical potential.

Even if a bodybuilder has been cursed with abysmal bodybuilding potential, he or she should never give up. Larry Scott, the first Mr. Olympia winner, is an excellent example of a bodybuilder who used determination and a scientific approach to his diet and training to overcome poor genetics. As a boy growing up in Idaho, Larry had wide hips, narrow shoulders, and an inability to gain muscle mass very quickly. Yet, Larry Scott persevered and over the years built a tremendous physique. Indeed, he became the greatest and most widely known bodybuilder of his era.

ORGANIZING YOUR OWN WORKOUTS

We can't go on forever making up your training routines, so in this section we will teach you how to do that for yourself. Here are six tried-and-proven rules to follow in making up your own workouts:

1. Never exceed the tolerances we have established at various training levels for number of workouts per week and total number of sets per body part. If anything, do *less* than the numbers of workouts and sets that we recommend.

2. Train your weakest body part(s) first in your workout, when your physical and mental energies are highest.

3. Never train your arms before your torso muscles, because this will aggravate the problem of your biceps and triceps being smaller and weaker than your lats, pecs, and delts.

4. Do your calf and/or abdominal workouts at the beginning of your routine as a warm-up to training the rest of your body.

5. Always do your forearm workouts last in your overall routine. Once your forearms have been fully pumped up it will be difficult for you to grasp a barbell or two dumbbells in your hands for other exercises.

6. Train your largest muscle groups toward the beginning of a workout, when you are most fresh. When fatigued toward the end of a workout, you will find it much easier to train a small muscle group like your triceps than it will be to give a good workout to your thighs or back. From largest to smallest, your muscle groups stack up like this: thighs, back, chest, calves, deltoids, triceps, biceps, abdominals, forearms.

SUPERSETS, TRISETS, GIANT SETS

One way advanced bodybuilders intensify their training for a muscle group—particularly during the precontest training cycle—is to compound two or more exercises for the body part with minimal rest between the movements. If two exercises are compounded, it's called a *superset;* if three movements are compounded, it's called a *triset;* and if four to six exercises are compounded, it's called a *giant set.*

Supersets can be done either for antagonistic muscle groups (e.g., barbell curls + pulley pushdowns = biceps + triceps; bench presses + lat pulldowns = pectorals + lats; or leg extensions + leg curls = quadriceps + hamstrings) or within a single muscle group (e.g., the pre-exhaustion supersets discussed in the next section). Trisets are usually done for muscle groups like the deltoids which have three aspects. As an example, you could do a deltoid triset consisting of side laterals (medial deltoid head), military presses (anterior head), and bent laterals (posterior head).

Giant sets can be done either for a single body part or for two antagonistic muscle groups. Here is a giant set strictly for the chest:

1. Bench Press (pectorals in general)
2. Cross-Bench Pullovers (rib cage expansion)
3. Parallel Bar Dips (lower/outer pectorals)
4. Incline Flyes (upper pectorals)
5. Pec Deck Flyes (inner pectorals)

And here is a giant set for two antagonistic muscle groups, the pectorals and latissimus dorsi muscles:

1. Bench Press
2. Chins
3. Incline Dumbbell Press
4. Seated Pulley Rowing
5. Cable Crossovers
6. Lat Pulldowns

In an intensity progression, supersets are a more intense training technique than merely doing straight sets. Trisets are the next rung up on an intensity ladder. And giant sets supply far more intense training than trisets. Actually, very few bodybuilders at even the international level use many giant sets in their training, and then they do so only to stimulate a muscle group or two that lags far behind the rest of the body.

Our Exact Precontest Routine

Generally, Val and I follow a four-day training cycle prior to contests, and when our schedules permit, we train together as often as possible. The body is split into three parts, which are trained on three consecutive days. The fourth day is set aside for complete rest, and the cycle begins again on the fifth day.

We prefer training in the morning, so we can devote the rest of the day to business, sunbathing, recreation, etc. We begin training at 6:00

a.m. and finish about 8:00 a.m. We never train more than once a day, and we always do stretching and a full warm-up before each weight workout.

Please note that our programs are changed periodically, but the following is a typical precontest routine that we use:

Workout I (Chest and Back)

Exercise	Sets	Reps
1. Abdominal Machine	6	variable
2. Lower Back Machine	3	10
3. Deadlifts	3	8-6-4
4. Incline Press	3	8
5. Chins	3	8
6. Machine Incline Flyes	3	8
7. T-Bar Rowing	3	8
8. Vertical Bench Press Machine	2	8
9. Lat Pulldowns	2	8
10. Vertical Flyes Machine	2	8
11. One-Arm Dumbbell Bent Rowing	2	8
12. Parallel Bar Dips	2	8
13. Pulley Rowing	2	8

Note: Brackets indicate exercises that are supersetted.

Workout II (Legs)

Exercise	Sets	Reps
1. Seated Twisting	6	100
2. Crunches	6	50
3. Standing Calf Machine	4	10
4. Front of Calf Raise	4	15
5. One-Leg Calf Raise	4	10
6. Leg Extension	3	10
7. Leg Curl	3	10
8. Leg Press (45-degree angle machine)	3	10
9. Hack Squat	3	10
10. Squat	2	20

Note: Bracket indicates exercises to be supersetted.

Workout III (Shoulders and Arms)

Exercise	Sets	Reps
1. Weighted Knee-Ups	6	10
2. Cable Bent Laterals	3	10
3. Dumbbell Bent Laterals	3	10
4. One-Arm Dumbbell Press	3	8
5. Seated Barbell Press	1	20
6. One-Arm Side Lateral Raise	5	8
7. Barbell Shoulder Shrugs	3	10
{ 8. Facedown Incline Curl	3	8
{ 9. Pulley Pushdown	3	8
{ 10. One-Arm Machine Curls	3	8
{ 11. One-Arm Triceps Extension	3	8
{ 12. Lying Pulley Curl	3	8
{ 13. Lying Dumbbell Triceps Extension	3	8
{ 14. Wrist Curl	5	15
{ 15. Reverse Wrist Curl	5	15

Note: Brackets indicate exercises to be supersetted.

PRE-EXHAUSTION

As we just mentioned, your biceps and triceps muscles are naturally smaller and weaker than your lats, pecs, and delts. Therefore, when you fail to complete a repetition at the end of a heavy set of bent rows, bench presses, or military presses, it's most likely that your arms gave out, not your torso muscles. That is why you should never do your arm workouts before training your torso—it simply aggravates this condition by making your arms even weaker and allowing you to train your torso even less hard than usual.

In order to get in an optimum chest, back, or deltoid workout, it's necessary to train your torso muscles with exercises that don't also require arm strength and/or use a technique called *pre-exhaustion.* By doing an isolation exercise like side laterals for your deltoids, you exhaust them and make your shoulder muscles temporarily weaker than your triceps. Then if you immediately superset this isolation exercise

with a shoulder movement using the arms (e.g., presses behind neck), you can push your pre-exhausted torso muscles to the limit before exhausting your arm muscles.

Here are several sample pre-exhaustion supersets that you can use to train your thighs (when squatting, your lower back will usually give out before your thighs), pectorals, lats, trapezius, and deltoids:

Thighs = Leg Extensions + Squats

Pectorals = Flyes + Bench Presses

Upper Pectorals = Incline Flyes + Incline Presses

Lower Pectorals = Decline Flyes + Parallel Bar Dips

Lats = Bent-Arm Pullovers + Lat Pulldowns

Trapezius = Barbell Shrugs + Upright Rows

Deltoids = Upright Rows + Military Presses

Deltoids = Side Laterals + Dumbbell Presses

Since a pre-exhausted muscle group will rapidly regain its strength (approximately 50% in 10–15 seconds), it's necessary to rest as little as possible between the two exercises of a pre-exhaustion superset.

QUALITY TRAINING

When a bodybuilder says that he or she is *pushing* during a precontest cycle, he or she is using a technique called *quality training.* When they are using quality training, all top bodybuilders gradually decrease the length of rest intervals between sets (from 45–60 seconds on an average in the off-season down to as little as 15–20 seconds). And while reducing the rest intervals, these champions endeavor to maintain use of maximum training poundages.

As we mentioned when discussing progression in Chapter 2, intensity can be increased by doing more sets, increasing the number of reps done for an exercise, or by *reducing rest intervals between sets.* Reducing set intervals is the quality training technique. By combining a fat-reduction diet with quality training, champion bodybuilders can develop the utmost in muscle mass and diamond-sharp cuts.

CIRCUIT TRAINING

One way of introducing quality into your training is to use a system called *circuit training*. In circuit training a series of 10–20 exercises—covering all parts of the body—is set up around a gym. Then a bodybuilder or athlete goes through this circuit one or more times with very little rest between stations. When done correctly, you should circuit train with only a long enough rest interval to move from one exercise station to the next.

Since so little rest is taken between exercises, circuit training with weights is an excellent way to build cardiorespiratory (heart-lung) endurance. And since this form of exercise also builds superior strength and a good degree of muscle mass, circuit training with weights is obviously one of the best all-around training methods that an athlete or fitness-minded individual can use.

We feel that every athlete and bodybuilder should try circuit training for at least 4–6 weeks. Here is a sample circuit that you can try for a few weeks (go through the circuit 3–4 times for your full workout):

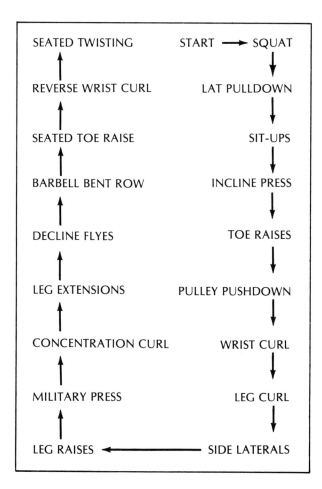

Val has used this type of circuit training routine extensively. She recommends it to all men and women, particularly those wishing to lose weight or increase athletic ability.

Another form of circuit training, popular during the mid-1960s, was called *PHA training*. "PHA" stands for "peripheral heart action." It is a system of short exercise circuits that stimulate peripheral heart action, or the use of skeletal muscle contractions to squeeze blood past one-way valves in the vascular system. Without such peripheral heart action, the human heart simply isn't strong enough to cope with circulating the amount of blood that each body must circulate. This system was popularized by Bob Gajda, the 1966 AAU Mr. America winner, against whom I competed in my early years of bodybuilding. PHA is actually a better way of using circuit training in a busy gym, because it depends on shorter circuits of only four to six exercises, which are much easier to organize and maintain with a lot of bodybuilders training in a gym than are circuits of up to 20 movements.

By designing circuits of four to six exercises, and choosing the exercises so you are stressing muscle groups by skipping all around the body, circulation is improved. When circulation is enhanced, the body's natural system of blood buffers (chemicals in the blood that neutralize fatigue toxins) can work more efficiently. As a result, you are able to do far more total sets in a workout than you can when using the normal *pump system* of training.

The following chart provides a sample PHA training program that you can use three non-consecutive days per week. Go through each series of exercises three to four times before moving on to the next series.

Series 1	Series 2
1. Squat	1. Standing Calf Machine
2. Upright Rowing	2. Hyperextensions
3. Sit-Ups	3. Press Behind Neck
4. Bench Press	4. Side Bends
5. Barbell Curls	5. Dumbbell Kickbacks
6. Bent Laterals	6. Reverse Curls

Series 3	Series 4
1. Leg Extensions	1. Seated Calf Raise
2. Barbell Shrugs	2. Lat Machine Pulldowns
3. Leg Raises	3. Incline Triceps Extensions
4. Incline Press	4. Seated Twisting
5. Concentration Curl	5. Side Laterals
6. Barbell Reverse Wrist Curl	6. Barbell Wrist Curl
Series 5	**Series 6**
1. Leg Curls	1. Donkey Calf Raise
2. Seated Pulley Rowing	2. Stiff-Leg Deadlifts
3. Pulley Pushdown	3. Decline Flyes
4. Knee-Ups	4. Lying Triceps Extension
5. Cable Crossovers	5. Dumbbell Wrist Curls
6. Incline Curls	6. Front Barbell Raises

No man or woman who has been following normal weight training or bodybuilding programs will have developed sufficient endurance to jump into a full program of circuit training or PHA training. This endurance must be developed over a period of four to six weeks, or even longer. On the foregoing PHA program, for example, you can comfortably do one trip through each of the first four or five series during your first workout. Then with each succeeding training session you can add a new series, or a repeat of an existing series, until you have worked up to completing the full program. You should use the same type of gradual break-in for regular circuit training.

OVERTRAINING

The human body has a limited capability for accepting volume of weight training exercise. And as a result, many bodybuilders overtrain. This usually happens when too much exercise is done, not when short, very intense workouts are taken.

How do you tell if you are overtrained? The following are seven symptoms of overtraining that you should be able to easily recognize:

1. Chronic fatigue
2. Lack of desire to train
3. Insomnia, or restless sleeping
4. Loss of appetite
4. Elevated morning pulse rate
6. Chronic muscle and/or joint soreness
7. Lack of gains in strength and/or muscle mass

Overtraining will result in a cessation of gains from your workouts, as we've just noted, so it's essential that you remedy the situation the minute you notice any of the above symptoms of overtraining. Begin by taking a one- to two-week layoff from training (layoffs are fully discussed in the next section). Then as soon as you resume training, be sure that it's on a new, shorter, and more intense routine. This method will jolt you out of your overtrained condition and start you back on the road to optimum gains from your bodybuilding training.

LAYOFFS

Even if you haven't overtrained, it's advisable to take periodic layoffs of 1–2 weeks duration from training. This rekindles your desire to train, gives minor injuries time to heal, and generally gives your body a rest period. After peaking for a major contest, you should always take a short layoff. And if you are not entering contests, you should still take a one-week layoff every 4–6 months. Doing so will actually enhance your rate of progress in bodybuilding.

STRENGTH WITHOUT BULK

Many athletes—particularly those in body weight economy sports like gymnastics and distance running—will be interested in gaining muscle strength without adding to their muscle size or body weight. This can be accomplished by doing very low repetitions (1–3) on basic exercises in two or three workouts per week. But to safely handle heavy weights for low repetitions, you must completely warm up, while still avoiding repetitions above three per set. Here is a typical strength-without-bulk set-and-repetition scheme for any exercise including the approximate percentage of your maximum best single effort for the exercise that you are using for a particular set:

Set Number	Percent	Reps
1	50%	3
2	70%	2
3	80%	2
4	90%	1–2
5	95%	1
6	95%	1
7	95%	1

Use this type of power-building workout only on basic exercises like the squat, deadlift, lat pulldown, bent rowing, shrugs, bench presses, incline presses, barbell curls, and lying triceps extensions. Actually, you could make up a very good strength-without-bulk routine using just these exercises and the foregoing sets/reps scheme. Do the workout two or three nonconsecutive days a week, and you'll quickly build great strength without significant added muscle mass.

VISUALIZATION

This statement may seem to be coming totally out of left field to you, but *creative daydreaming can turn you into a better bodybuilder or athlete.* By regularly visualizing yourself the way you would like to be, you can program your subconscious mind—almost like programming a computer—to automatically make choices that will allow you to achieve the image you have visualized. It's a psychological process called *self-actualization,* and it's at the heart of psychocybernetics and related self-achievement techniques.

To make visualization work well for you, it's necessary to visualize yourself vividly and realistically as you will one day look and act. This visual image must look as clear and detailed as a movie image. So you are visually projecting an image on a screen that's on the inside on your eyelids. Visualize every muscle, every vein, every hill and valley of muscular definition. Make the image as real as possible.

For visualization to optimally condition your subconscious mind, it must be done regularly and at a time when your body is relaxed and your mind free from the day's distractions.

These criteria can best be met each night in the relaxed minutes just before you fall asleep. Simply set aside 10 or 15 minutes for visualization each night, faithfully conjure up your future image, and you will be well on the way to having a superb physique.

Visualization can also help you in your everyday life. You can achieve anything you can vividly visualize, so give visualization a trial as a method of improving your study or work habits, interpersonal relationships, etc. If you visualize every day, you'll be surprised at how quickly this technique can help you to become a superman or superwoman.

BODYBUILDING DRUGS

No topic has provoked as much heated discussion in recent years in bodybuilding as that of using drugs—particularly anabolic steroids—to aid progress in building muscle. Whether or not you as a bodybuilder decide to use drugs to help your body reach peak condition will be a matter of personal choice. We do, however, make these generally accepted recommendations and comments regarding bodybuilding drug usage:

1. No drug should be taken without the direct supervision of a physician, or without the preliminary tests recommended before commencing use of a particular drug.

2. Every drug presents some degree of risk to a patient using it. Become thoroughly acquainted with these risks before you decide to use any drug.

3. Generally speaking, it is foolish to use any type of bodybuilding drug prior to achieving a national level of competition.

4. Women should never use steroids or androgenic drugs.

Anabolic Steroids

At the end of World War II, anabolic steroids were developed as aids to help former concentration camp inmates and POWs build their weight back to normal. In many cases, these unfortunate people had become so weakened that they were unable to regain normal body weight without the use of steroids. Today, these drugs are used for a similar purpose in geriatric medicine.

Anabolic steroids are artificial male hormones with the anabolic (muscle building) characteristics enhanced and their androgenic (male secondary sex characteristics producing) factors suppressed. Because of their muscle-building properties, steroids gained favor among weight lifters and bodybuilders during the early 1960s. Today athletes in virtually every sport use steroids. Farmers have even used steroids such as *stilbestrol* to fatten up their cattle and poultry for market.

Steroids definitely build muscle, but they have numerous side effects, which are accentuated by lengthy and/or high-dosage use. Here are the recognized side effects of anabolic steroids:

1. Liver and kidney damage
2. Possible liver, kidney, and prostate cancer
3. Premature closure of bone growth centers in pubertal and pre-pubertal youths, resulting in a stunting of growth
4. Water retention and high blood pressure
5. Masculinization and clitoral enlargement in women
6. Testicular atrophy and decrease of libido in men
7. Acne and hair loss
8. Increased aggression
9. Osteoporosis (a weakening of the bones through loss of bone calcium)
10. Death

Obviously, the last of these contraindications from anabolic steroids—although rarely encountered—is one that should be seriously pondered by anyone who considers taking anabolic steroids.

One mistake novice bodybuilders make is using steroids to *build* muscle mass. Experienced male bodybuilders use them only for six to eight weeks prior to competition to maintain mass while on a strict diet. The problem here is that, even though gains can be made rapidly on steroids, they are lost just as quickly once off steroids. And as soon as mass begins rapidly to dissipate, there is a huge temptation to go right back on the drugs, accentuating side effects with their prolonged use.

This loss of muscle mass occurs in all male bodybuilders who stop using steroids. To illustrate why this happens, arbitrarily assume that your body naturally produces 100 units of testosterone, the male muscle-building hormone. And with 100 units of testosterone you can build 100 units of strength and 100 units of muscle mass each month. Artificially adding 20 units to your testosterone level via anabolic steroids increases your muscle mass and strength gain by 20%. This is a tremendous occurrence for most bodybuilders, but unfortunately, adding 20 units to your testosterone levels only increases your 20% gain *temporarily*. Your body has something called a *negative feedback mechanism*. This mechanism senses fluctuations in testosterone levels—as well as levels of other chemicals—in the bloodstream and adjusts natural testosterone production to maintain the 100-unit level. When you add 20 units, the negative feedback mechanism senses this increase and begins to reduce natural testosterone production.

Two or three weeks later, your natural testosterone output will have been reduced to only 80 units, so with the added 20 units from steroids your body will be back to its normal 100-unit level. When this happens, a vicious cycle begins: bodybuilders begin to progressively increase their steroid dosages to keep ahead of the rate at which their body ceases to produce testosterone.

Continuing with our example, assume that after 6–8 weeks of steroid usage, your body has reduced its testosterone output to 50 units. Once off steroids, your body will require from 6–8 weeks to return its testosterone production to normal (100 units). During that period you will be producing far less testosterone than normal. And as a result you will not only be unable to maintain the new degrees of strength and muscle mass that you've developed, but most likely you'll be unable to maintain your normal 100-unit strength and muscle mass levels. The resulting quick loss of mass and strength is what induces many bodybuilders to stay on steroids for long periods of time, multiplying these drugs' dangers.

The most commonly used anabolic steroids are Dianabol, Anavar, Winstrol, Deca-Durobolin, and Therabolin. The first three of these are taken orally, and the last two are administered via intramuscular injection.

Androgenics

These are pure testosterone preparations of various sorts that some bodybuilders take. Supposedly, testosterone will have a beneficial anabolic effect and will give the physique a *hard* look. Unfortunately, this is only partly true, and in the long run many of the side effects of anabolic steroids will be experienced to drastically accentuated degrees in individuals who take testosterone.

Compared with steroids, testosterone actually has a very low anabolic index. And it retains far more water in the body than anabolic steroids, so it's difficult to believe that it can make the male body look harder. Most bodybuilders become hyperaggressive while on testosterone. We have actually seen several bodybuilders on testosterone get into fist fights in the gym in the middle of their workouts.

It would be disastrous for a woman to take testosterone, because its injection is a fundamental part of sex change procedures. Very quickly a woman on testosterone will develop a deep voice and begin growing a beard. And most of the side effects from steroids and androgenics are irreversible in women.

Stimulants

When energy is dragging while on a tight precontest diet, many bodybuilders resort to using such energy stimulants as amphetamines and cocaine. This is quite foolish, because these chemicals actually eat away at muscle tissue. They also have a high addiction potential. What intelligent bodybuilder wants to lose muscle mass and become dependent on a drug?

Appetite Depressants

These include amphetamines, cocaine, and other drugs. Again, they eat up muscle mass and can be addictive. It seems to us that it is more safe and sensible to simply use self-discipline in following a diet.

Thyroid Supplements

These drugs include dessicated beef or porcine (hog) thyroid glands, synthroid, and nu-merous others. They are intended to speed up the body's metabolism and burn off fat, revealing maximum muscular definition. Unfortunately, thyroid drugs are indiscriminate in choosing the type of tissue to burn up. They metabolize muscle as well as fat, resulting in a muscular—but stringy looking—physique. Again, it's better just to follow a strictly disciplined diet for a longer period of time. You will get just as cut up, but will retain most of your muscle mass.

Analgesics

Analgesics are pain killers, which are generally acceptable for use, as long as they don't mask pain so completely that you can further injure yourself. Traditionally, pain killers like aspirin have been used by bodybuilders. Recently, however, many bodybuilders and other athletes have begun to use DMSO (dimethyl sulfoxide) as a safe and effective painkiller. A mild breath odor is the only side effect noted from DMSO usage, and it reduces pain quite efficiently.

DOUBLE-SPLIT ROUTINES

While we don't personally use double-split routines, many champion bodybuilders do. We caution you, however, against trying a double-split until you have reached the national or international level of competition. Training on a double-split routine is extremely fatiguing, and it's probable that anyone with less than 3–5 years of steady training behind him will overtrain quite quickly using such an intense training routine.

There are two primary advantages to using a double-split routine. First, it allows you to do shorter—and, therefore, more intense—workouts. This is a distinct advantage when you are on a tight precontest diet and your energy levels are low. To work out for an hour, rest six or eight hours, then train for another hour is far easier energy-wise than doing one long 2–2½-hour workout. And you'll get far more intense work done in two hours on a double-split than in a single two-hour workout.

A second advantage to using a double-split

routine is that it speeds up your metabolism and makes it easier to get cut up for a competition. Whenever you do several workouts a day—whether they are bodybuilding sessions or aerobic workouts—your metabolism will gradually increase over what it is when you train only once a day. And the more speedy your metabolism, the better will be your ultimate degree of muscular definition.

The easiest type of double-split routine to follow involves doing your major workout in the morning and a concentrated calf-and-abdominal session in the late afternoon or evening. Even this simple double-split will allow you to train each muscle group with a little greater intensity.

One of the most frequently used double-split routines involves two workouts on Mondays, Wednesdays, and Fridays and a single workout on Tuesdays, Thursdays, and Saturdays. Sunday, of course, is a rest day. Here is an example of this type of double-split routine:

M-W-F (a.m.)	M-W-F (p.m.)
Chest	Shoulders
Back	Arms
Calves	Abdominals

Tu-Th-Sa (a.m. or p.m.)
Thighs
Calves
Forearms
Abdominals

Another step up the intensity ladder can be made by following a full, double-split routine with two workouts a day six days a week. Here is an example of such a routine:

M-W-F (a.m.)	M-W-F (p.m.)
Chest	Back
Shoulders	Forearms
Calves	Abdominals

Tu-Th-Sa (a.m.)	Tu-Th-Sa (p.m.)
Thighs	Biceps
Calves	Triceps
Forearms	Abdominals

Very few bodybuilders do this, but it's even possible to train three, four, or five times a day. In this case a bodybuilder usually trains only one body part per workout, which allows him or her to train very intensely for 20–30 minutes. This can be effective if you have the temperament and financial resources to follow through on such workouts. Laura Combes, the first American Women's Bodybuilding Champion (a title she won in 1980), trains like this just prior to competing.

CHEATING

In Chapter 2 we advised you to do all of your exercises in very strict form. There is, however, a way to use *cheating* to make a set of any exercise even more intense than usual. The key to effectively cheat in your training is to utilize it to make an exercise *harder* to do, not easier. Merely using your legs and back to swing up a few reps in the barbell curl isn't productive.

The best way to cheat is to first take a set to *failure,* which is to the point where you can no longer complete a full strict repetition. In the barbell curl, for example, you might get a rep up high enough for your arms to be bent at 90-degree angles, but you aren't able to take it any higher. This is the point at which you should cheat just enough to get the barbell or other apparatus past the sticking point. Then you should slowly lower the weight back to the starting point, strongly resisting its downward momentum every inch of the way.

By doing two or three such cheating reps at the end of a set you will be able to force a muscle to work much harder than usual by pushing it past its normal failure point. And pushing a muscle this much harder forces it to grow more quickly in both mass and strength. Be sure at all times, however, to cheat only to make an exercise harder on a muscle group, not to take resistance from it.

FORCED REPS

Forced reps are another training technique that will allow you to push your muscles past the point of ordinary failure, and thus to add intensity to a set of any exercise. Assuming you are using 100 pounds for barbell curls and can do

Boyer demonstrates strict form, left, and "cheating" form, right.

six strict repetitions with it, when you miss your seventh rep, it means only that you could curl 100 pounds for reps one through six, but that you couldn't curl 100 pounds on your seventh rep. You won't be able to curl it, because your biceps will have become too fatigued. Even fatigued, though, your biceps might be able to curl 95 or 90 pounds.

The easiest way to instantly make your barbell weigh 5-10 pounds less is to have your training partner lift upward on the middle of the

bar just enough to allow you to force out another repetition. For your first forced rep, he or she should pull up on the bar with a force of only 5-10 pounds. Your muscles will be more fatigued on a second rep and your partner will have to pull up 10-15 pounds. On a third forced rep your partner will need to pull up 15-20 pounds.

Usually two or three forced reps will be sufficient in a set of any exercise. When you first begin using forced reps, you should do them on only one set of one basic exercise for each muscle group. Then gradually add to the number of forced rep sets you do for each body part. But be careful with these forced reps, because you'll overtrain on them if you do too many sets with forced reps. Used judiciously, however, forced reps will definitely accelerate your bodybuilding results.

I have used forced reps extensively in my workouts, and recommend them to anyone who desires to increase his or her strength and muscle mass. Forced reps were primarily responsible for most of my recent professional competition wins and high placings in pro shows.

NEGATIVES

Many years ago, German physiologists discovered that the lowering (negative phase) of an exercise had as much—if not more—potential for developing strength and muscle mass as the positive (raising phase) of a movement. Weight lifters, powerlifters, and bodybuilders went through a phase in the early 1970s in which they used pure negative movements in their exercises. But in pure negatives, two training partners must lift up a very heavy weight so the trainee can resist the lowering phase of the movement, which wore out training partners faster than they could be found! Therefore, bodybuilders have had to adapt negative training for either self-use or for limited use with a single training partner.

Self-use of negative reps can be done by *emphasizing* the negative half of a movement in exercises that can be done on machines. Take toe raises on a standing calf machine as an example of how this can be done. Load up the machine with a weight that you can use to complete 12–15 repetitions. Do five full-range reps to warm up. Then on the sixth rep, go up as high as possible. Lift your right foot free from the toe block so all of the weight is on your left foot. Slowly lower back to the start, emphasizing the negative portion of the movement for your left calf by putting double the usual weight on it. At the bottom, place your right foot on the toe block and go up to the top again on both feet. This time, lower yourself on your right foot. Alternate feet until your calves are fully fatigued. You will have then done a

negative emphasis set of toe raises for your calves, bombing them much harder than when doing a normal set just to failure.

Another way to use negatives is to have a training partner help you to extend a set past the point where you would normally take it with forced reps. Using barbell preacher curls as an example of how this is done, load a weight on the bar so it's heavy enough that you can do five or six full-range positive and negative reps before muscular failure on the exercise. Once you've failed to complete a rep, your training partner can assist you to force out two or three more reps. After those forced reps, however, your biceps will be so fatigued that further forced reps won't do them much good. This is where negatives come in. At the end of the forced-reps series, your partner will lift the weight up for you, after which you mightily resist the negative phase of the movement for two or three purely negative reps.

This type of set will put the torch to your biceps like nothing you've ever done, but it will also give your biceps an unprecedented growth stimulus. When you train this hard within a single set, you will probably need to do no more than five or six total sets per workout for each muscle group. Even this small number of sets, as long as they are maximally intense, will totally fatigue most muscle groups.

Overall, negative reps done at the end of a series of forced reps can best be performed on basic exercises like barbell preacher curls, regular barbell curls, bench presses, decline and incline presses, chins, lat pulldowns (with the legs restrained), barbell triceps extensions, leg curls, leg extensions, and toe raises. We wouldn't recommend such negatives done on sets of squats, because a set of squats done to failure is so fatiguing that it would be much too painful to do forced reps as well as negatives at the end of the set.

Negative emphasis reps can be done only on machines in which you can remove one hand or leg from the movement without destroying the symmetry of an exercise. Obviously, you couldn't remove one hand from a barbell when doing curls, because that side of the barbell would crash to the floor. On a curling machine, however, you could remove one arm with no danger. You can do the same on all calf machines, leg curl and leg extension machines, and most Nautilus machines.

PEAK CONTRACTION

Physiologically, a maximum number of muscle fibers are being called into play only when a muscle is fully contracted. This can easily be observed in how much the middle of your biceps muscle humps up when you flex your arm. And it's logical that you can most fully stimulate a muscle to increase its size and strength if you can place maximum stress on it when the muscle is fully flexed and with most of its fibers in a contracted state.

Unfortunately, many exercises do not allow you to place full resistance on a completely contracted muscle group. In barbell curls, for example, maximum resistance is felt on your biceps only when your forearms are at a 90-degree angle to your upper arms. By the time you finish the curl and your biceps are fully flexed, there is very little stress being placed on your biceps. If you bend over until your torso is parallel to the floor and hang your arms straight downward, however, you can do a peak contraction barbell concentration curl in which most of the resistance is still on your biceps when they're fully contracted.

In general, most exercises done on machines—and particularly those done on Nautilus apparati—allow you to take full advantage of peak contraction training. As an example, machine curls are done on an apparatus that swivels on a cam, so full resistance is placed on the biceps over every inch of the rotary movement of the curl. Nautilus also gives *balanced* rotary resistance in which the weight is made heavier or lighter at points along the curl—or other exercises—in which the biceps are naturally stronger or weaker. This is accomplished by varying the radius of the cam, rather than having one that is truly circular.

There are also numerous free-weight or other apparatus exercises that allow you to use peak contraction training. Some of these are toe

By bending over and performing curls, Boyer causes peak contraction throughout the movement.

raises on standing and seated calf machines, hanging frog kicks, hanging leg raises, leg extensions, leg curls, cable crossovers, pec deck flyes, dumbbell side laterals, cable side laterals, dumbbell bent laterals, cable bent laterals, front raises, barbell or dumbbell concentration curls, dumbbell kickbacks, and wrist curls done standing erect and with a barbell held behind the thighs.

CONTINUOUS TENSION

One very good technique for bringing out peak muscle density for a competition is called *continuous tension*. In this technique you attempt to feel the resistance provided by a barbell, dumbbells, or exercise machine over the full range of movement of an exercise. This is accomplished by moving the weight slowly over the range of movement of the exercise. Of course at the start and finish of most movements, very little tension is on a muscle group. Then, tension should be supplied by contracting antagonistic muscle groups (e.g., the triceps supply tension to the biceps when you are doing concentration curls).

When you use continuous tension, you will be able to handle only 70%–75% of the weight you usually use for an exercise. Still, you will be working your various muscle groups quite hard with continuous tension, regardless of the weight used. We generally use *quality training, continuous tension,* and *peak contraction* for 4–6 weeks prior to competing. We use *cheating, forced reps, negatives,* and *pre-exhaustion* more in the off-season when we are trying to add new muscle mass to our bodies.

ISO-TENSION CONTRACTION

This is a relatively new nonresistance training technique that will do much to enhance muscularity and muscle density if used four or five weeks prior to a competition. Iso-tension contraction involves merely flexing each muscle maximally hard in a variety of positions for 8–10 repetitions of 5–10 seconds duration. Such iso-tension workouts must be done daily—or even twice a day—for best results. We've found it best to practice the iso-tension contraction

technique in conjunction with our regular posing practice during the weeks leading up to a competition or exhibition.

Correctly used, iso-tension contraction will greatly harden your muscles. It will also give you much better control over your muscles as you pose them. With enough practice of iso-tension contraction—as well as regular posing—you will eventually be able to control every muscle striation in your contest-ready physique. For example, every pectoral striation can be controlled, so under tension your chest muscles will look like slabs of wax that have been repeatedly scratched by a large, very angry cat.

A NOTE TO WOMEN

Women weight trainers and bodybuilders often ask Val about the effects of weight training and other forms of exercise on menstruation, pregnancy, and menopause. All forms of exercise—but particularly weight training and bodybuilding—have very beneficial effects on these functions.

If you are cramping badly during your menstrual cycle, there seems to be no reason why you should work out. But scientific studies have demonstrated that just one or two months of regular exercise will dramatically reduce the severity of menstrual cramps. And if you also make sure that you supplement your diet with calcium, magnesium, potassium, and other chelated minerals, you can almost completely eliminate menstrual cramping. Double up on all minerals beginning four or five days before the onset of your period and continue taking high dosages until two or three days after your period is finished.

In some cases, exercise and diet can lead to a complete cessation of menstrual periods. Essentially, any woman who reduces her body fat to less than 8% or 9% of her total weight will not menstruate until her body's fat content returns to normal. There is nothing dangerous about this unless you take a cessation of your period as a sign of infertility. Unfortunately, this would be a very unreliable form of birth control.

Scientific investigators have also concluded that women who are in top physical condition have fewer chances of pregnancy complications and have easier labor than sedentary women. And, at your obstetrician's discretion, you can continue weight training and other forms of exercise while pregnant. This will make carrying and delivering your baby a joy. Just as one example, strong back muscles—gained through weight training—will prevent the lower back discomfort experienced by many heavily pregnant women.

As with menstruation, the distressing symptoms of menopause (depression, wild mood swings, etc.) can be alleviated altogether or greatly reduced by exercising regularly and following a healthy, balanced diet. When going through menopause, it's especially important to follow a low-fat diet that is supplemented with calcium, vitamin B complex, multiple vitamins, and chelated multiple minerals. And if you experience difficulty sleeping, try taking 3–5 tryptophane tablets 30 minutes before going to bed. As we mentioned earlier, tryptophane— one of the eight essential amino acids—is a natural tranquilizer with no side effects. It's available in all health food stores.

GET WITH IT!

We have now taught you all you'll ever need to know to use weight training and bodybuilding to rapidly improve your health, fitness, physical appearance, and general lifestyle. With over 30 years of collective experience in weight training and bodybuilding, we've personally experienced all of these benefits and seen thousands of other men and women experience these benefits as well. So, we can't recommend working out with weights enough. It's a superb form of exercise.

At this point, we can't lead you any further. We can't do the workouts for you. Only you can do your workouts, but only *you* will benefit from the hard work you do and the disciplined lifestyle you follow. We're throwing the ball to you. Catch it and run hard. We're behind you all the way!

Glossary

Aerobic Exercise—Long-lasting, low-intensity exercise which can be carried on within the body's ability to consume and process enough oxygen to support the activity. The word *aerobic* literally means "with air." Typical aerobic exercise activities are running, swimming, and cycling. *Aerobic* exercise leads to cardiorespiratory (heart-lung) fitness.

AFWB—The American Federation of Women Bodybuilders, the sports federation responsible for administering women's amateur bodybuilding in America. The *AFWB* is affiliated internationally with the IFBB (see **IFBB**).

AMDR—The Adult Minimum Daily Requirement(s) for various nutrients, as established by the U.S. Food and Drug Administration.

Anaerobic Exercise—High-intensity exercise that exceeds the body's aerobic capacity and builds up an oxygen debt. Because of its high intensity, *anaerobic* exercise can be continued for only a short time. A typical *anaerobic* exercise would be full-speed sprinting on a track.

APC—The American Physique Committee, Inc., the sports federation responsible for administering men's amateur bodybuilding in America. The *APC* is affiliated internationally with the IFBB (see **IFBB**).

Bar—The iron or steel shaft which forms the handle of a barbell or dumbbell. Barbell *bars* vary in length from about four to seven feet, while dumbbell *bars* are 12 to 16 inches long. *Bars* are usually one inch in diameter, and are often encased in a revolving sleeve (see **Sleeve**).

Barbell—This is the basic piece of equipment for weight training. It consists of a bar, sleeve, collars, and plates (see **Bar, Sleeve, Collar,** and **Plates**). The weight of an adjustable *barbell* without plates averages five pounds per foot of bar length. The weight of this basic *barbell* unit must be considered when adding plates to the bar to form a required training poundage (see **Poundage**). *Barbells* in large gyms are usually *fixed*, with the plates welded to the bars in a variety of poundages. These poundages are designated by numerals painted on the sides of the plates of each *barbell*.

Bodybuilding—A subdivision of the general category of weight training (see **Weight Training**) in which the main objective is to change the appearance of the human body via weight training and nutrition. For most men and women, *bodybuilding* consists merely of reducing a fleshy area or two and/or building up one or two thin body parts. In its purest form, *bodybuilding* for men and women is a competitive sport both nationally and internationally in amateur and professional categories.

Bodysculpting—This term is occasionally used in a feminine context to mean *bodybuilding*.

BMR—The Basal Metabolic Rate, or the natural speed at which the body burns calories when at rest to provide its basic survival energy needs.

Circuit Training—A specialized form of weight training which develops body strength and aerobic endurance simultaneously. In *circuit training,* a trainee plans a circuit of 10–20 exercises covering all of the body's major muscle groups, then proceeds around this circuit in order while resting minimally between sets. Many athletes use *circuit training* to improve their strength, muscle tone, and overall endurance in one type of workout.

Collar—The cylindrical metal clamp used to hold plates (see **Plates**) in position on a barbell. Usually these *collars* are secured in place with a *set screw* threaded through the *collar* and tightened against the bar with a wrench. *Inside collars* keep plates from sliding inward and injuring a trainee, while *outside collars* keep the plates from sliding off the end of the bar. For safety, you should never lift a barbell unless the *collars* are tightly fastened in place.

Couples' Competition—Also called "Mixed Pairs' Competition," this is a new form of bodybuilding competition in which male/female teams compete against each other. Couples' competition is becoming very popular with bodybuilding fans all over the world.

Cut—A term used to denote a well-defined bodybuilder (see **Definition**). Usually this is a complimentary term, such as in saying, "He's *really* cut up for this show!"

Definition—This term is used to denote an absence of body fat in a bodybuilding competitor, so that every muscle is fully delineated. When a competitor has achieved ideal *definition,* his or her muscles will show striations, or individual fibers along a muscle (see **Striations**). *Definition* is also called *muscularity*.

Density—The hardness of muscle tissue, denoting complete muscularity, even to the point where fat within a muscle has been eliminated.

Dumbbell—This is simply a shorter version of a barbell, which is intended for use in one hand, or more commonly with *dumbbells* of equal weight in each hand. All of the principal parts and terminology of a barbell are the same for a *dumbbell*.

Exercise—Used as a noun, this is the actual

weight training movement being done (e.g., a bench press or a squat). An *exercise* is often called a *movement*. Used as a verb, *exercise* is the act of undertaking physical work recreationally and for health reasons with weight training or any number of other forms of *exercise* (e.g., running, playing softball, etc.).

Flexibility—A suppleness of muscles and connective tissue which allows any man or woman to move his or her limbs and torso over a complete—or even exaggerated—range of motion.

Hypertrophy—The growth in size and strength of any skeletal muscle.

IFBB—The International Federation of Bodybuilders, which was founded in 1946 by Ben and Joe Weider. It is the parent international federation overseeing worldwide men's and women's amateur and professional bodybuilding. More than 115 national bodybuilding federations are affiliated with the *IFBB,* making bodybuilding the world's seventh most popular sport.

Intensity—The degree of difficulty built into weight training exercise. *Intensity* can be increased by adding resistance (see **Resistance**), increasing the number of repetitions done of an exercise (see **Repetition**), or by decreasing the rest interval between sets (see **Rest Interval** and **Set**). The greater the *intensity* of bodybuilding exercise placed on a muscle, the greater will be that muscle's rate of hypertrophy.

Judging Rounds—In the internationally accepted IFBB system of bodybuilding judging, three *judging rounds* are contested, plus a final posedown in which the top five contestants compete in a free posing manner for added points. In Round One, each bodybuilder is viewed standing relaxed facing his/her front, left side, back, and right side to the judges. Round Two consists of a set of standardized compulsory poses, while Round Three is devoted to creative individual free posing to each contestant's own choice of music.

Lifting Belt—A leather belt 4–6 inches wide at the back that is worn around the waist to protect a trainee's lower back and abdomen from injuries. The six-inch belt can be used in training, but only the four-inch belt can be used in weight lifting competition (see *Weight Lifting).*

Mass—The size or fullness of muscles. Massiveness is highly prized in bodybuilding competition, especially for men.

Muscularity—Another term for definition (see **Definition**).

Nutrition—The various practices of taking food into the human body. Bodybuilders have made a science of *nutrition* by applying it to add muscle mass or to totally strip fat from their bodies to achieve optimum muscle definition.

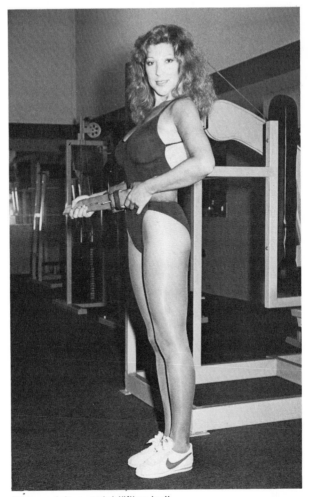
Val models a weightlifting belt.

Olympic Barbell—A highly specialized and finely machined barbell used in weight lifting competition. An *Olympic barbell* weighs 20 kilograms (slightly less than 45 pounds) and each of its collars weighs 2½ kilograms (5.5 pounds).

Olympic Lifting—A form of competitive weight lifting included in the Olympic Games since the revival of the modern Olympics at Athens in 1896. Until 1972 this form of weight lifting consisted of three lifts: the press, snatch, and clean and jerk. Because of officiating difficulties, however, the press was dropped from use following the 1972 Olympic Games, leaving the snatch, and the clean and jerk as the two competitive Olympic lifts.

PHA—An abbreviation for "peripheral heart action," in which each skeletal muscle acts as an auxiliary heart by milking blood past one-way valves in the arterial system. Without *PHA*, the heart itself would have difficulty circulating blood. *PHA* is also a term assigned to a system of circuit training (see **Circuit Training**) in which shorter series of five or six exercises were used in circuits.

Plates—The flat discs pierced with holes in the middle that are fitted on barbells and dumbbells to increase the weight of these apparati. *Plates* are made of cast metal or vinyl-covered concrete. They come in a wide range of graduated weights from as little as 1¼ pounds to over 100 pounds each.

Poundage—The actual weight of a barbell, dumbbell, or weight machine resistance used in an exercise.

Powerlifting—A form of competitive weight lifting using three lifts: the squat, the bench press, and the deadlift. The sport is contested nationally and internationally. Unlike in Olympic lifting, special women's competitions are held in *powerlifting*.

Proportion—A competitive bodybuilding term referring to the size relationships between various body parts. A contestant with good *proportions* will have no over- or under-developed muscle groups.

Pyramidding—A technique of gradually increasing weights lifted while decreasing the number of reps performed. For example, in doing three *pyramidded* sets of an exercise, you might begin the first set with 100 pounds and do 8 reps, then 110 pounds for 6 reps, and finish with 120 pounds for 4 reps.

Repetition—Often abbreviated as *rep*, this is each individual full cycle of an exercise from the starting point of the movement to the midpoint and back again to the starting point. Usually, series of several *repetitions* are done for each exercise.

Resistance—As with *poundage*, this is the actual weight being used in an exercise.

Rest Interval—The pause between sets of an exercise (see **Set**) during which the worked muscles are allowed to partially recuperate before the succeeding set is begun. *Rest intervals* vary from as little as 10–15 seconds to as much as five minutes. An average *rest interval* should be 60 seconds.

Olympic barbell and squat rack.

Routine—Sometimes called a *program* or *schedule,* this is the complete accumulation of exercises, sets, and reps, done in one training session. A routine is usually repeated two or three times each week.

Set—A distinct grouping of repetitions, followed by a brief rest interval and another *set.* Usually, several *sets* are done for each exercise in a training program.

Sleeve—A hollow metal tube fitted over the bar of a barbell. The *sleeve* allows a bar to rotate more easily in your hands. Ordinarily, grooved *knurlings* are scored in the *sleeve* to aid in gripping the barbell when the hands have become sweaty during a training session.

Spotters—Training partners who stand by as a safety factor to prevent you from being pinned under a heavy barbell. *Spotters* are particularly necessary when you are doing bench presses.

Steroids—Prescriptive, artificial male hormones that some bodybuilders use to increase muscle mass. Anabolic *steroids* are very dangerous drugs, however, and we do not recommend that anyone use them.

Stretching—A type of exercise program used to promote body flexibility. It involves assuming and then holding postures in which certain muscle groups and body joints are stretched.

Striations—This is the ultimate degree of muscle definition. When a muscle mass like the pectoral is fully defined, it will have myriad small grooves across it, almost as if a cat had repeatedly scratched the wax surface of a statue's pectoral muscles. These tiny, muscular details are called *striations.*

Supplements—Concentrated vitamins, minerals, and protein, usually in tablet/capsule or powder form. Food *supplements* are widely used by competitive bodybuilders, weight lifters, and athletes to optimize their overall nutritional programs.

Symmetry—In competitive bodybuilding par-

lance, this is the shape or general outline of the body, as if it was seen in silhouette. *Symmetry* is enhanced in both male and female bodybuilders by a wide shoulder structure; a small waist-hip structure; small knees, ankles, and wrists; and large muscle volumes surrounding these small joints.

Vascularity—The appearance of surface veins and arteries in any bodybuilder who has achieved a low level of body fat. Women tend to have *vascularity* primarily in their arms, while male bodybuilders can have surface *vascularity* all over their bodies.

Weight—Another term for *poundage* or *resistance.* Sometimes this term is used to generally refer to the apparatus (barbell, dumbbell, etc.) being used in an exercise, versus the exact poundage being utilized.

Weight Class—So that smaller athletes are not overwhelmed by larger ones, competitive

bodybuilding and weight lifting utilize *weight classes.* In women's bodybuilding, the classes (at the time of writing this book) were: under 52½ kg. (114 lbs.) and over 52½ kg., while men's bodybuilding weight classes are set at: 70 kg. (154 lbs.), 80 kg. (176 lbs.), 90 kg. (198 lbs.), and over 90 kg. or heavyweight. Power-lifting and Olympic lifting are contested in a much wider variety of weight classes. Converted to pounds from international metric equivalents, these are: 114, 123, 132, 148, 165, 181, 198, 220, 242, 275, and over 275 pounds.

Weight Lifting—The subdivision of weight training in which men and women compete in weight classes both nationally and internationally to see who can lift the heaviest weights for single repetitions in prescribed exercises. Two types of *weight lifting—*Olympic lifting and *powerlifting—*are contested.

Weight Training—The various acts of using resistance training equipment to exercise the body or for competitive purposes.

Workout—A weight training session. "To work out" is to undertake a weight training session.

Index